Higher
Social Justi

SRHE and Open University Press Imprint

Higher Education and Social Justice

Andy Furlong and
Fred Cartmel

JUBILEE
CAMPUS
LRC

Society for Research into Higher Education
& Open University Press

Open University Press
McGraw-Hill Education
McGraw-Hill House
Shoppenhangers Road
Maidenhead
Berkshire
England
SL6 2QL

email: enquiries@openup.co.uk
world wide web: www.openup.co.uk

and Two Penn Plaza, New York, NY 10121-2289, USA

First published 2009

Copyright © Furlong and Cartmel 2009

A catalogue record of this book is available from the British Library

ISBN-13: 978-0-33-522362-6 (pb) 978-0-33-522361-9 (hb)
ISBN-10: 0335223621 (pb) 0335223613 (hb)

Library of Congress Cataloging-in-Publication Data
CIP data applied for

Typeset by RefineCatch Limited, Bungay, Suffolk
Printed in the UK by Bell and Bain Ltd, Glasgow.

1005825824

Mixed Sources
Product group from well-managed forests and other controlled sources
www.fsc.org Cert no. TT-COC-002769
© 1996 Forest Stewardship Council
FSC

The *McGraw·Hill* Companies

Education is our most powerful tool for social justice.
(John Denham, Secretary of State for Innovation,
Universities and Skills, *The Times*, 2008: 22)

Contents

List of figures

List of tables

Acknowledgements

The origins of this book lie in three related projects funded by the Joseph Rowntree Foundation, 'Socioeconomic disadvantage and access to higher education', 'Losing out? Socioeconomic disadvantage and experience in further and higher education' and 'Graduates from disadvantaged families: Early labour market experiences', each of which led to the publication of a report. Alasdair Forsyth worked as Research Fellow on these projects and was co-author (with Andy Furlong) of the first two reports: we are pleased to acknowledge his contribution to the projects. Alasdair also conducted the interviews for the first two projects while Maggie Lawrence interviewed for the final project.

Charlie Lloyd of the Joseph Rowntree Foundation was involved throughout the programme of work and made a substantial contribution to the success of the projects, not least in supporting our case for continued funding! We would also like to thank those who contributed through membership of the advisory group to one or more of the projects: Andy Biggart, Frank Corrigan, Bryony Duncan, Barbara Graham, Cathy Howieson, Vivian Leacock, Kevin Lowden, Robert Macdonald, Ian Neish, Janice Pattie, Sheila Riddell, Paul Teasdale, John Tibbitt and Chris Warhurst. Interview tapes were transcribed by Kay Devlin, Olive Kearns and Flora Smith. Mike Osborne of the Department of Adult and Continuing Education and Denis Smith of the Department of Management at Glasgow University read and commented on each of the chapters and made valuable suggestions for improvement. Finally, we would like to thank the young people who participated in the project, especially those who made themselves available for interview.

1
Higher education and social justice

Higher education is challenged to continue advancing the equity cause, not as an add on but as an integral element in its broader intellectual, cultural, social and economic purposes . . . Higher education has a key role in advancing the values of justice, democratic life and their wider dissemination in society. This is not a separate, free standing, theoretically disposable role, but a central or core value, part of the enduring concept of education as universal enlightenment, civic development and personal fulfilment.

(Skilbeck 2000: i)

Introduction

In many western countries, including the UK,[1] higher education has recently become part of the normal, taken-for-granted experiences of the middle classes. More than four in ten young people in the UK now enter higher education and the government wants to see that figure rise to 50 per cent in England and Wales by 2010.[2] The youth labour market has all but disappeared and with a serious decline in the number of quality jobs available to early school-leavers, there is strong pressure to remain in education and collect more qualifications in order to secure the most advantageous economic returns. Recognizing the difficulties encountered in the labour market by early school-leavers, the UK government is currently debating proposals to raise the minimum leaving age from 16 to 18. While targets relating to levels of participation in higher education may be desirable and may be expressed in terms of overall averages, the experience of higher education has been, and remains, highly stratified and, to an extent, 'intended to differentially empower its recipients' (Ross 2003a: 22). In some communities a university education is neither aspired to nor expected and, in any case, many of those who are brought up in poor areas leave school without the sorts of qualifications that would facilitate progression.

Higher education in all parts of the UK is highly stratified with strong divisions in institutional status, ease of access and employment prospects applying within the 'traditional' university sector and the ex-polytechnics and colleges of education. In many ways the patterns of stratification found in higher education today closely parallel the types of division that were found in secondary education prior to the roll-out of comprehensive schools. In the UK in the 1950s and 1960s, children were largely educated alongside peers from similar socio-economic backgrounds. In the main, those from the working classes were educated in secondary modern schools and channelled towards early labour market entry and jobs in the semi-skilled and unskilled sectors of manufacturing industry. In contrast, those from the middle classes tended to be educated in grammar schools where they were prepared for university or for white-collar careers in the expanding service sector. These stratified modes of delivery were reflected in expect-ations. For many working-class children, a grammar school education was neither desired nor anticipated, just as today university education remains off the radar in many poor neighbourhoods.

These forms of segregation were not always interpreted by the public as being unjust or as perceived as organizational forms that were guaranteed to protect middle-class advantage while limiting the numbers of working-class recruits to elite positions. The divisions were justified in terms of 'academic ability' and large sections of the public accepted the view that a relatively small proportion of the population had the potential to benefit from either a grammar or a university education, and the aptitude to work in professional or higher managerial occupations was viewed as something pos-sessed by a small minority. For the bulk of the population, aptitude and ability were assessed at the end of primary school on the basis of an examin-ation known as the 11 plus. For the wealthy, it was possible to avoid potential failure by purchasing access to a private education which smoothed access to higher education, even for those with little ability or aptitude.

The objectivity of the 11 plus examination was sometimes challenged (there was growing unease, for example, with an examination that required girls to obtain higher marks to be awarded a pass) and there were debates about the proportion of young people who had the potential to be able to benefit from advanced education and about the most appropriate age to make selections that would have a far-reaching impact on future life chances. While selection at age 11 has become far less common, until relatively recently there was a broad acceptance of the idea that university education should be highly selective. Many regarded university as only suitable for academic high-flyers who had provided evidence that they had the interest and potential to immerse themselves in a subject and learn from leading specialists in the field who were often engaged in cutting-edge research. University education was unashamedly about elitism and therefore necessa-rily entailed some form of selection both at the point of entry and in terms of the type of secondary education that would help prepare young people for the rigours of academic life. With a widespread appreciation that a university education opened doors to the most prestigious and lucrative sectors of the labour market and provided access to privileged lifestyles, political parties of the left and right were aware of the importance of convincing the public that educational selection was made on the basis of criteria that were perceived as fair and legitimate: even in the face of powerful evidence that few young people from working-class families managed to secure access.

This book is concerned with the provision of equal opportunities in higher education, but takes the view that any apparent political commitment to introduce the types of reform that would result in a socially just system of opportunities are, at best, superficial and at worst designed to placate or mislead the working classes. Indeed, those who make the decisions that count, whether in politics or in the education sector itself, frequently have an interest in maintaining the injustices that will ultimately protect their own offspring. A political acceptance of the need for a system of selection that is open and impartial runs counter to practice which has continued to allow the wealthy to purchase a privileged education for their offspring and even provides tax benefits and grants charitable status to private schools so as to ensure private education is accessible to the middle classes.

In this opening chapter we explore the contradictions between social justice, wider access and the maintenance of elite and middle-class advantage. We suggest that the history of higher educational expansion is underpinned by a desire to balance the contradiction between fairness and protectionism, masked by an ongoing 'debate' about the need to maintain academic standards. We begin by looking at what is meant by social justice, before moving on to debate the purpose of higher education in late modern societies. Through a brief history of the expansion of universities in the UK we highlight the debates about wider access that have underpinned policy change and show how decisions made during a period of rapid expansion created the two-tier system that continues to underpin the class-based stratification of higher education today.

Social justice: what is it?

Policy debates relating to the expansion of higher education, especially those taking place following the publication of the Dearing Report (1997), often made explicit reference to the need to build a system based on the principles of social justice. But social justice is not a term that is widely used by the public at large and may be open to misinterpretation. So what is meant by social justice? Essentially social justice relates to the principle that every effort should be made to ensure that individuals and groups all enjoy fair access to rewards. It is about creating a 'more equitable, respectful and just society for everyone' (Zaijda et al. 2006: 13, quoted in Brennan and Naidoo 2007: 26). However, social justice is not necessarily about equality; it can be about providing equal opportunities to access an unequal reward structure. All advanced Western societies pay lip service to the principles of social justice, even though most have consistently failed to provide the basic preconditions for a socially just society. In a society committed to the ideals of social justice, it is recognized that fair treatment and equal opportunities for everyone can only be brought about by imposing restrictions on the behaviour of some individuals or groups. And this is where the problem lies: the provision of opportunities to members of less advantaged groups is uncontroversial; restricting the opportunities of the middle and upper classes has proved to be a political bullet that few governments have been prepared to bite – not least because it would involve the imposition of restrictions on opportunities of the families of politicians and on those with whom they identify and may alienate a large segment of the electorate.

For John Rawls, a socially just society will be reflected in 'a fair system of co-operation over time, from one generation to the next' (1971: 14). The family is the key to what he regards as an unjust natural lottery through which rewards are distributed in a manner that can only be described as arbitrary. As he puts it:

> The principle of fair opportunity can only be imperfectly carried out, at least as long as the institution of the family exists. The extent to which natural capacities develop and reach fruition is affected by all kinds of social conditions and class attitudes. Even the willingness to make an effort, to try, and so be deserving in the ordinary sense is itself dependent upon happy family and social circumstances.
>
> (1971: 73–4)

Rawls argues that social justice requires the equal distribution of 'all social primary goods – liberty and opportunity, income and wealth' (1971: 303) unless some form of unequal distribution actually advantages the 'least favoured'. His idea of social justice involves more than the equal opportunity to access unequal positions. He also recognizes that any reward system that provides advantages to those who display superior performance is likely to result in a form of distribution that is essentially arbitrary and favours those with pre-existing advantages. In other words, while some may regard talent, ability or effort as attributes that merit reward, to provide differential privilege on the basis of something like ability (which is randomly distributed) or effort (which is conditioned by family circumstances) is likely to result in the reproduction of inequalities and therefore runs counter to the idea of social justice.

In terms of access to education, those who accept Rawls' position would object to any form of selection, whether selection for different types of secondary education, for ability streams within a comprehensive school or access to an elite university – unless the process could be shown to result in greater benefits for all. In the absence of such evidence, a Rawlsian position would hold that any attempt to select on the basis of merit or ability will inevitably result in a system that rewards privilege of birth and, ultimately, legitimizes differentials.

In his 1958 satire *The Rise of the Meritocracy*, Michael Young traces the tension between merit and privilege back to the 1870s and, in futuristic speculation, projects forward in time to 2033. He describes early attempts to invigorate a sluggish economy by injecting merit into an occupational structure in which the top positions were monopolized by the sons of the wealthy, who often lacked both intellect and diligence, and observes the various efforts of the elite to protect privileges for their own families in the face of a perceived meritocratic onslaught. While free universal educa-tion (between the ages of 5 and 15) had become established by 1944 and universities had supposedly opened their doors to all who were 'capable of benefiting' following the Robbins Report in 1963, the upper and middle classes were always able to find new ways of protecting access to superior forms of educational provision. Indeed, while governments have made various attempts to improve provision for the working classes, they always lacked the courage to abolish the private schools, to remove their charitable status, or to intervene directly to ensure universities functioned as more than finishing schools for members of the upper middle classes. The long-standing and deeply entrenched shame of the British Labour Party has been the widespread patronage by elected Members of Parliament (including cabinet ministers) of the private educational sector. The decisions of con-temporary Labour politicians to educate their children in the private sector have been well quoted in the press and used to cast doubt on their commit-ment to a more egalitarian system (while around 7 per cent of the popula-tion are privately educated, nearly a third of MPs have attended private schools (Sutton Trust 2005a)). A recent Labour Education Minister, Ruth Kelly, for example, enrolled her son in a private school: a decision that was defended by politicians in her own and in opposition parties on the basis that a parent has to put the needs of their own child first. The lack of personal commitment to universal state provision among members of the Labour Party has been long-standing, as noted by Sir Hartley Shawcross in 1956:

> I do not know of a single member of the Labour Party, who can afford to do so, who does not send his children to public school, often at a great sacrifice – not for snobbish reasons or to perpetuate class distinction, but to ensure his children get the best.
>
> (Shawcross, quoted in Young 1961: 64)

The commitment to social justice is fundamentally undermined by struc-tures, such as private schools, that facilitate the maintenance of advantage. Private schools, though, are the tip of an iceberg of educational privilege which in Britain today covers a range of schools that enjoy some form of separation from the mainstream state sector while continuing to derive large parts (if not all) of their income from the public purse. From church schools to the new city academies, what is referred to as the 'grant maintained sector' effectively imposes restrictions on entry, selecting pupils with characteristics that they regard as desirable. The existence of a selective grant maintained sector alongside an open state sector is hard to reconcile with the principles of social justice. Tempting though it might be for those with power to protect their privilege, an education system that provides the preconditions for equality of opportunity has to be built on structures that restrain those who would seek to use education as a mechanism through which socio-economic advantages can be protected. As the liberal philosopher L.T. Hobhouse advised, social improvement is conditional upon the imposition of restraints on the powerful:

> The first condition of universal freedom . . . is a measure of universal restraint. Without such restraint some men may be free but others will be unfree. One man may be able to do all his will, but the rest will have no will except that which he sees fit to allow them.
>
> (Hobhouse 1964: 17)

In a British context, the idea of abolishing all forms of selection, both at the compulsory and post-compulsory levels, is not currently on the agenda of any of the mainstream political parties. Indeed, providing access to university to anyone who has the inclination to undertake tertiary level study, irrespective of prior attainment, seems outlandish. Free access would tend to be regarded as undermining academic standards while removing the option of paying for education outside of the public sphere would be regarded as a curtailment of liberty. Yet both principles have operated without major problems in other parts of Europe and in some countries are regarded as closely linked to social justice. In the UK, social justice in higher education is seen as involving little more than widening access to groups that have traditionally been excluded. Reflecting contemporary concerns about social injustice, there have been discussions about the way in which the growth in participation has meant increasing the middle-class representation rather than extending opportunities to the working classes and minority groups, and particular disquiet about the monopolization of places in the top universities by the upper middle classes.

On a practical, day-to-day level, social justice is not a concept that preoccupies many families, but the concerns of parents regarding the future prospects for their offspring are all underpinned by their understandings of what social justice means. The problem is that interpretations of social justice are contextual and inextricably linked to socio-economic positions: as Sen (1992) notes, the acceptance of egalitarian principles are widespread, but there can be major conflicts between groups with regard to the forms of equality that they value. For working-class families, it may involve the provision of opportunities to improve standards of living, enhanced security and the opportunity to develop potential. Increasingly this may include opportunities to engage in some sort of tertiary education as they come to perceive job security and comfortable lifestyles to be linked to educational outcomes. For the middle classes a socially just system is one that guarantees their 'right' to a quality education for their children. A sound basic system of education would be one that respected middle-class values and ensured that their offspring were qualified not just to progress to tertiary education, but had excellent chances of entering one of the better universities and an outside chance of being accepted for an elite course of study. At the basic level, the middle classes demand that their children are provided with a standard of education that would protect from serious downward mobility (and, for additional protection, the adoption of fiscal policies that would safeguard the transfer of resources between generations). For the upper classes, expectations are higher and social justice may be interpreted as keeping open channels which ensure that privilege is passed on to the next generation. In a modern context, this tends to be linked to the ability to pay for a private education where their offspring is spared the need to mix with the hoi polloi and subsequently assured access to higher education within one of the elite universities.

Importantly, these differing interpretations of social justice directly affect the demands that ultimately shape educational provision: a provision that is just as highly stratified as the class-based demands of the electorate. The aspirations and expectations of young people who are in the process of applying to higher education are shaped by what Bourdieu (1977) would refer to as their 'habitus' and therefore become part of the process of social reproduction. This process of assumptive stratification and its impact on the social justice of the higher educational process will be discussed at length in subsequent chapters.

What is the purpose of higher education?

There has been a long-standing tendency to separate debates about social justice from discussions about the purpose of higher education and of the best way of delivering so as to meet agreed aims. For traditionalists, a university is essentially a semi-monastic community of scholars primarily pursuing knowledge for its own sake with no necessary regard for the utility of their endeavours (Newman 1907). For others, the purpose of higher education is to provide a context where the most able individuals can be prepared for demanding occupations requiring advanced skills, specialized knowledge, and the ability to solve problems within a disciplinary frame-work. Trow suggests that three distinct priorities can be identified in systems of higher education: (1) an 'elite' system which gives priority to shaping a ruling class and preparing students for privileged positions; (2) a 'mass' system which prepares students for a broad range of technical and elite roles; and (3) a 'universal' system aiming to prepare a 'whole population' for rapid economic change (2006: 243). In *Higher Education in the Learning Society* (1997), Dearing suggests that there is a widespread consensus on the key objectives of higher education. For Dearing, higher education is required to meet the demand for a highly qualified workforce, to satisfy public demand for high level education and to provide a world-class research capacity. Osborne offers a slightly broader statement of objectives including:

the economic imperatives created by global competition, technological change and the challenge of the knowledge economy, individual responsibility and self-improvement, employability, flexibility of institutions and individuals, social inclusion and citizenship.

(2003: 6)

If we scratch the surface though, it quickly becomes clear that views about the purpose of education often contain competing objectives. From the government's perspective, the provision of higher education is strongly linked to international competitiveness and economic prosperity. In the modern global economy, what David Blunkett[3] referred to as 'intellectual capital' is crucial and the future position of the country is linked directly to investment in human capital. In this context, the Leitch Report (2006) appears to have signalled an increased emphasis on utilitarianism in higher education and a greater willingness to engage employers in the process through a demand-led approach. Accepting the main tenets of the Leitch Report, the incumbent Education Secretary, Ruth Kelly, issued a directive in which she accepted the desirability of some sectors of higher education as being 'partly or wholly designed, funded and provided by employers'.

The Exchequer will obviously have an eye on future returns through taxation of professional employees, will be aware of the reduced demand for state benefits from a highly skilled citizenry and will realize that a strong university sector makes a significant contribution to the balance of payments through attracting large numbers of foreign students and by providing knowledge that might stimulate the development of new, exportable, products or services. In other words, for some stakeholders, higher education may be regarded primarily as an industry rather than as a social institution (Maassen and Cloete 2006).

Increasingly politicians have come to accept that the role of a modern university is not simply to produce world-class research, make significant contributions to the economic well-being of the country or to enhance the national skill base, universities also have an important role to play in underpinning social justice. Recognizing that universities, especially the older universities, significantly under-perform when it comes to the provision of equal opportunities, recent changes in funding regimes (see Chapter 3) have been accompanied by the establishment of an Office of Fair Access[4] which has the responsibility to monitor access inequalities and set targets for improvement which must be met before an institution is allowed to increase tuition fees.

While academic staff in the universities often recognize the desirability of widening access and their contribution to skill enhancement, often their prime purpose may be to do with a desire to push back the frontiers of knowledge, to stimulate student interest in their discipline, to be able to set their own intellectual agendas and to be able to contribute to the development of their subject. They might even reject or attempt to subvert attempts by educational managers or politicians to try and treat their activities as part of a profit-making enterprise with set output targets and 'objective' performance measurements, while some will not even recognize the desirability of promoting wider access. Some academics manage to combine fairly traditional views about the purpose of universities as communities centred around theory and ideas, while holding the more radical view that universities represent a 'site of social and cultural interpenetration' responsible for nurturing the development of an 'educated public' (Barr 2008) prepared to become involved in civil society and capable of holding politicians to account.

For students and their families, the purpose of higher education may be seen in terms of individual utilitarianism. Higher education may be regarded as linked to future prosperity, security and quality of occupational opportunities. It may be thought of as an investment which generates long-term economic and social rewards, which have a major impact on future lifestyles and protects against downward social mobility. For some, there is an additional reward derived from the advanced study of a subject in which they have a strong interest and which may be linked to the chance of employment in an occupation offering the possibility of working within the framework provided by that discipline. For others, the subject may be quite instrumental; it may have been chosen as an area of personal academic strength or simply as offering a route to a degree requiring least effort on the part of the student. Indeed, some students may simply regard university as a mechanism that allows them space to develop leisure-focused lifestyles for three or four years.

These different views about the purpose of higher education mean that for many stakeholders social justice is not a primary concern. Indeed, while the current structure of higher education in the UK (and in many other countries) is underpinned by a system of selection that provides advantages to some while restricting the opportunities of others, politicians clearly do not feel under pressure to prioritize the abolition of inequalities associated with selection. Even among left of centre political parties, there is little serious debate about reforming higher education in ways that conform to Rawlsian principles. Indeed, commitment to some form of selection based loosely around the idea of prior attainment or demonstrable potential is deeply entrenched, even though selection may impede progress to the establishment of a socially just system. In some countries, the principles of social justice are more central to higher education policies. In the Scandinavian countries, for example, very explicit links are made between higher education and social justice. In Denmark, a key objective of higher education is to 'assist in creating and developing a sustainable, economically sound, democratic society where few have too much and even fewer too little' (Dearing 1997: Appendix 5, section 10). Higher education is seen as creating the preconditions for a fairer society, reducing economic and social differentials and ensuring that citizens are equipped to participate fully in an inclusive democracy. In the UK, social justice tends to be more of what Skilbeck would refer to as an 'add on' rather than as an integral component (2000: i).

Increasing participation, widening access

The period between the end of the Second World War and the late 1960s/ early 1970s saw the university landscape change quite radically. Britain emerged from the First World War with just 15 universities (only 10 of which were in England). They were unashamedly elitist, catering for a small section of the population with women excluded from many institutions and courses. Cambridge, for example, did not allow women to graduate until 1947, although they were permitted onto certain courses of study. In the immediate post-war period there was some expansion with a few new university colleges founded (which later gained full university status) and the establishment (in 1956) of ten Colleges of Advanced Technology, largely through the merger of regional colleges. The Colleges of Advanced Technology were granted degree-awarding powers and later gained full university status (Ross 2003a). Table 1.1 list the important policy landmarks in higher education.

In many respects, prior to 1945, higher education in the UK was simply not fit for purpose either in terms of providing the human resource for economic expansion or for laying the foundations for a more socially just or democratically inclusive society. A university education was virtually the exclusive preserve of the upper classes, many of whom were not particularly bright. With just 2 per cent of young people progressing to university, the Barlow Report (Ministry of Education 1946) on scientific manpower went as far as suggesting that about half of those gaining entry did not possess an 'adequate intelligence' (quoted in Young 1961: 35) and argued that when it came to access, 'the scales are weighted today in favour of the socially eligible' (quoted in Ross 2003a: 30). Barlow drew attention to the fact that intelligence tests conducted during the Second World War showed that around 5 per cent of the overall population achieved scores which were at least as high as the top 50 per cent of the student body (who represented just 1 per cent of the general population).

Information made available through the widespread testing of the population as part of the war effort revealed the level of untapped potential as well as highlighting the extent to which privileged dullards occupied key leadership positions. As Young put it, 'every child from an elementary school who became an officer in the Hitler war . . . was an argument for educational reform' (1961: 32). The case for expanding higher education while ensuring that the most able young people were offered the opportunity of a university education gained widespread acceptance, but estimates about the depth of the pool of potential varied. For Barlow, the brightest 5 per cent were capable of benefiting from higher education, and he argued that it was important to ensure that universities recruited the most able rather than the most privileged young people.

Student numbers increased slowly in the post-war years – reaching about 7 per cent by the early 1960s, but university largely remained 'a finishing school for people of wealth and standing' (Gordon et al. 1991: 233). The

Table 1.1 Policy landmarks in higher education

Year	Official document	Outcome
1946	Barlow Report	Highlights inequalities in access and wastage of talent.
1960	Anderson Report	Leads to the introduction of maintenance grants and abolition of fees
1963	Robbins Report on Higher Education	Establishes principle that higher education should be available to all who are qualified and able to benefit.
1965	'A Plan for Polytechnics and Other Colleges' White Paper	Establishment of 30 Polytechnics, controlled by local educational authorities
1978	Special courses in preparation for entry to higher education	Department of Education and Science invites local educational authorities to establish courses with a focus on getting adults and ethnic minorities into vocational areas such as teaching and social work.
1992	Further and Higher Education Acts	Abolition of binary divide provides opportunities for polytechnics to acquire university status.
1997	Dearing Report on Higher Education	Proposal to increase participation rates, particularly among under-represented groups, partly paid for by contributions towards fees by working graduates.
1998	Teaching and Higher Education Act	Abolition of maintenance grants, extended system of loans, 'upfront' tuition fee of £1,000 introduced.
2003	'The Future of Higher Education' White Paper	Appointment of Fair Access Regulator to oversee arrangements for widening access by universities. 'Upfront' fees abolished with pay-back arrangements deferred until after graduation.
2004	Higher Education Act	Universities able to charge differential fees subject to approval by the Fair Access Regulator, but forced to make provision for students from less advantaged families.
2006	Leitch Report	Emphasizes the importance of developing 'economically valuable skills' within a demand-led system that involves employers.

issue of widening access was not seriously addressed until 1963 when the Robbins Committee put the development of higher education firmly on the political agenda. For Robbins, economic growth depended on the rapid expansion of higher education, and an enhanced rate of participation was seen as necessary and desirable. Robbins also established the principle that higher education 'should be available to all those who are qualified by ability and attainment to pursue them and who wish to do so', irrespective of social background or gender (Committee on Higher Education 1963: 8): his estimate of this qualified 'pool of ability' was judged to be in the region of 17 per cent. Although justified on economic grounds, the expansion of higher education was clearly regarded as a means of providing a more equal opportunity structure and of reducing the impact of class and gender-based barriers to access (Finch 1984).

The earlier acceptance of the Anderson Report (Ministry of Education 1960) meant that the cost of tuition was met in full by the state and students were provided with means-tested grants to cover living costs. The availability of grants effectively removed one of the main barriers to participation for those whose parents lacked the means to support their offspring while they attended higher education. The level of grant made available to those from poorer families was set at a level which was just about generous enough to allow students to live independently and to study at a university away from their home region without having to engage extensively in paid work in term time. The value of the grant was seriously eroded during the 1980s and subsequently abolished in favour of loans in 1998.

The growth of participation in higher education in the aftermath of Robbins was brisk, with a 50 per cent rise in participation between 1963 and 1968 (Reay et al. 2005). The changes that were introduced also laid the foundations for the mass system that began to emerge in the 1970s and 1980s as a result of changes in secondary education and an increase in qualified school-leavers, cultural changes that stimulated social and economic aspirations and a growing demand for educated workers. In the immediate post-Robbins era, the most significant advances in social justice were changes in the gender balance of participants in higher education rather than improvements in class differentials. In the 1960s, almost seven in ten qualified males entered higher education, compared to just over four in ten qualified females (Ross 2003b). By 2004/05 female students were in a clear majority (Self and Zealey 2007).

Driven by the Robbins' principle of increasing provision to meet the demands of those qualified to benefit, between 1969 and 1973, 30 polytechnics were established to help provide places for the expanding student population. The polytechnics largely provided for 'local students, local needs and vocational education' (Davies et al. 1997: 4) leaving the university sector to maintain its traditional focus on elite education and research. In effect, the Robbins' reforms helped facilitate wider access to higher education, but also (inadvertently and apparently to his surprise) laid the foundations for a binary system in which most working-class students were not offered an education in the established (or even the newly established) universities, but were largely allocated places in the polytechnics which were controlled by local authorities and provided with inferior funding.

In many ways, the emergence of a binary system of higher education at this particular point in time was surprising. Comprehensivization was firmly on the political agenda and the Secretary of State for Education, Tony Crosland, had declared an intention to 'destroy every fucking grammar school in England' (Crosland 1982: 148, quoted in Ross 2003b: 46). As with secondary education, the danger of a differentiated system of higher education is that the educational experiences of different social classes become highly stratified. With entry to higher education governed by qualifications gained at school, the middle classes tended to qualify for older universities which set the higher entry tariffs while the inferior secondary education offered to the working classes meant that they were 'pushed' towards the polytechnics. With the polytechnics tending to offer more vocational courses, they also proved popular with working-class students seeking courses with clear links to the world of work. Indeed, working-class families sometimes had a familiarity with the technical colleges out of which the polytechnics emerged and parents may have taken courses at these institutions as part of an apprentice-style training.

Although Robbins had envisaged the creation of more universities through mergers of local colleges and by bringing them under central control, the local authorities proved hostile and Crosland came to accept the views of his senior civil servants that the most effective way forward was to recognize the distinct contribution made by the local colleges in providing vocational education focused strongly on the needs of industry (Ross 2003b). For Crosland, the polytechnic sector was 'not inferior, but different' (Crosland 1982: 159). There was also an issue of trust. Universities enjoyed considerable autonomy in respect of courses offered and the government was concerned that the programmes that academics thought appropriate to develop would not necessarily be those that politicians had identified as being in the public interest (Shattock 2006).

Over time, the binary divide in higher education blurred. In 1988, responsibility for the polytechnics was centralized and in 1992 responsibility for universities and polytechnics was handed to the newly created Higher Education Funding Council, and polytechnics were encouraged to apply for permission to call themselves universities. Yet despite the adoption of common titles, in popular discourse a distinction is still made between the 'old' and the 'new' universities, sometimes referred to as post-1992 institutions. The 'new universities' have yet to gain the status of the established sector and there are very strong differences in the social backgrounds of the students. To paraphrase Osborne (2003), just one part of the higher educational sector, the post-1992 universities, has taken responsibility for the lion's share of the widening participation remit. The differences between the 'old' and the 'new' sectors are recognized and celebrated by some who argue that the 'new' university sector has been responsible for some radical reforms that have transformed the university experience by making it more friendly to 'non-traditional' students. One ex-vice-chancellor of a new university, for example, recently argued (with some justification) that 'the major innovations of the 1970s and 1980s came from the polytechnic sector – access, widening participation, emphasis on teaching and learning, broadening the curriculum, the focus on the student experience' (*Times Higher Education Supplement* 2007a: 32).

The building of the 'plate glass' universities, largely on greenfield sites, in the 1960s, the expansion of the ancient and 'red brick' universities and establishment of polytechnics from the late 1960s (granted university status from 1992), and the creation of a number of new universities from colleges from the 1990s onwards, not only created more capacity, but also led to a greater diversity of provision (Table 1.2). In 1960, less than 200,000 UK students participated in higher education on a full-time basis: by 2006, this had increased to well over a million (Figure 1.1). The increased diversity of provision meant that the undergraduate life in 'new' universities was very different from that of the typical student experience in the older universities. These differences extended from the approaches and expectations of lecturing staff, to the social mix of students and their opportunities to engage with each other outside of the classroom. The tradition of a residential experience, established by the 'ancients' and replicated by the modern 'greenfield' universities, never became widespread in the 'new' universities and gradually became less common in most city institutions as students and their parents looked for ways of reducing costs. For some commentators, residence has been regarded as central to a rounded and effective university experience (Silver 2007) and as a mechanism that facilitates socialization between members of different social classes, ultimately facilitating processes of socio-economic mobility.

While the increased supply of places in higher education helped cater for frustrated demand, the rapid increase in participation from the 1970s onwards was driven by a number of factors. These included the widespread introduction of comprehensive education, higher levels of secondary participation resulting in a greater pool of qualified applicants and the stimulation of demand for higher education from under-represented groups,

Table 1.2 Chronology of university foundation

Typology	University	Date
Ancient universities	Cambridge	1209
	St Andrews	1410
	Glasgow	1450
Civic and 'red brick' universities	Manchester	1880
	Sheffield	1905
	Bristol	1909
'Plate glass' universities	Warwick	1961
	Kent	1965
	Essex	1965
New or 'post-1992' universities	Manchester Metropolitan	1992
	Abertay	1994
	Cumbria	2007

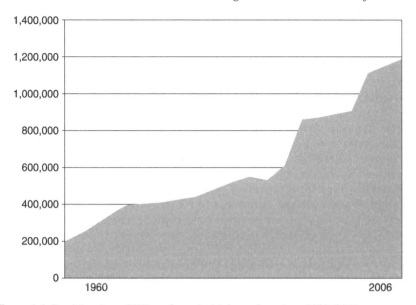

Figure 1.1 Participation of UK students in higher education, 1960–2006

Source: Derived from the Dearing Report (1997), Ministry of Education (1962 and various other years) and the Higher Education Statistics Agency (2008).

particularly women and mature students. Attitudes towards education also changed as university degrees became associated with entry to a broader range of occupations and were no longer so closely associated with privileged upbringings.

Clearly, changes in the labour market, particularly the demise of the manufacturing sector and the increased demand for professional, managerial and administrative positions in the service sector, had a major impact on the demand for higher education. The possession of a degree increased career opportunities and enhanced pay and conditions in a growing range of occupations. Yet it became clear that increasing participation did not necessarily result in *wider* participation. As we shall show in the next chapter, the main winners were the middle classes.

Calls for genuinely wider access gained prominence in the late 1990s following the Dearing Report. Universities started to be asked to account for the social imbalance of their intakes and ministers began to 'name and shame' institutions that over-fished from the pool of privilege. In the modern context, wider access is about increasing access to higher education among under-represented groups, particularly those from working-class families and from minority groups. It is also concerned to ensure that these groups make significant inroads to subject areas and disciplines where they have traditionally been poorly represented. The issue, however, is that social justice in admissions policies does not simply involve granting access to under-represented groups, it has to involve turning away applicants from privileged families who have stronger credentials (Young 1961; Watson 2006).

Conclusion

Despite the huge growth in participation in higher education in the post-war era, the creation of new institutions and greater diversity of students attending higher education, the system remains highly stratified. In the next chapter we shall look in some detail at the extent of inequality and at some explanations regarding processes of stratification. In this chapter we have highlighted some of the contradictions between wider access and social justice, suggesting that the various stakeholders have different interpretations of the purpose of higher education, of access and of what social justice entails in the context of higher education. Essentially, in the UK, a weak variant of social justice underpins public and political debate. Fairness is rarely seen as involving the restriction of opportunities for privileged groups.

While there are benefits in supporting a diverse range of offerings in higher education, providing opportunities for people with a wide range of interests and with preferences for a variety of pedagogic approaches, it is important that some routes are not regarded as inferior in status or funding. This is difficult to achieve and many countries have ended up with stratified systems of higher education. In the following chapters we will explore some of the ways in which institutional structures restrict opportunities for less advantaged students and thwart efforts to establish a more socially just system in which all are able to develop their potential and pursue their interests, unrestricted by socio-economic disadvantage.

2

Unequal access

A constant factor in all Member States [of the European Union] for which data are available, is that while absolute participation rates may have increased for all socio-economic levels, the relative rates have barely changed. The likelihood of attending a university or pursuing tertiary studies remains far higher for those from higher socio-economic levels.

(Green et al. 1999: 204, quoted in Skilbeck 2000: n.p.)

Introduction

Higher education is no longer the exclusive preserve of the upper middle classes, but the significant expansion that has occurred has not resulted in fair access. Even though almost one in two young people in the UK will spend time in higher education, the experience remains highly structured: those from poorer families and from certain minority groups are largely excluded and when they do manage to gain admittance, they are unlikely to be allowed access to elite universities or courses with clear routes into desirable professions such as medicine or law. Perhaps we should not be surprised, Will Hutton has expressed great scepticism at the idea that universities like Oxford and Cambridge may significantly reduce the numbers of entrants from the private schools so as to achieve fairer patterns of access. Describing the top universities as the 'closed shop' of the British middle classes, he argued that the role of these institutions is to act as 'gatekeepers to the elite, recruiting students whose background and bearing suggest they will make good elite members' (Hutton 2006: 27). Indeed, Hutton goes as far as arguing that Oxford and Cambridge fulfil a function similar to that of China's Communist Party schools and the US Ivy League.

In this context it is important to appreciate that in many countries in the past, radical changes have occurred in the provision of educational opportunities without this having an appreciable impact on class-based differentials.

In the UK, Halsey and colleagues (1980) showed that the introduction of free secondary education in 1944 did little to expand opportunities for grammar school education among the working classes, largely because the middle classes were successful in monopolizing places. Similarly, there has been a debate as to whether the introduction of comprehensive schools had much of an impact on the performance of working-class pupils (e.g. Heath 1987). After drawing similar conclusions about the benefits of educational expansion in Ireland, Raftery and Hout (1993) proposed a theory of 'maximally maintained advantage'. Essentially their argument was that educational expansion tends to occur in a way that results in little change in class-based differentials until a 'saturation point' is reached. In other words, applied to higher education, it could be suggested that working-class gains will only occur once places have been provided for virtually all members of the middle classes. The Scandinavian experience seems to support this idea (Parjanen and Tuomi 2003).

In the first part of this chapter we describe inequalities in access to higher education, both in terms of overall levels of entry among different social and economic groups as well as patterns of entry to different segments of the higher educational market place (referred to by Iannelli (2007) as horizontal stratification). With evidence clearly showing poor entry prospects and a stratification of experience in which those with fewest resources are placed in the least desirable sectors, the working classes mix with students from similar backgrounds in concrete ghettos that resemble their inner city secondary schools. In the second part of the chapter we begin to focus on the reasons why non-traditional students have made such poor inroads and identify some of the key mechanisms that help restrict access to higher education.

Mapping inequality

Although the numbers of young people entering higher education have increased among all social groups, expansion has been achieved with very little impact on the overall social distribution of entrants. This is true of the UK as well as most other developed countries (Blondal et al. 2002; Baum and Payea 2004; Haveman and Wilson 2007). Commenting on trends in the social class composition of the higher educational sector, the Office for National Statistics' publication, *Social Trends*, states quite bluntly that 'the gap in participation rates between those from manual and non-manual classes has *increased* over the last 40 or so years' (Summerfield and Gill 2005: 36: our emphasis). In other words, the middle classes have managed to retain – and even increase – their advantages despite the shift from an elite to a mass system of higher education which has resulted in increased odds of attendance for all social classes. Supporting this view, Blanden and colleagues (2005) show that graduation rates of children with parents in the lowest income quintile only increased very slightly since the 1970s while those with parents in the highest income quintile more than doubled. 'The clear conclusion is that the expansion of higher education in the UK has bene-fited those from richer backgrounds far more than poorer young people' (Blanden et al. 2005: 12).

Using figures from the England and Wales Youth Cohort Study, Iannelli (2007) shows that between 1989 and 2002, working-class entry into higher education increased from about 4 per cent to around 14 per cent. Over the same period, participation from the managerial and professional classes rose from around 19 per cent to about 37 per cent. In other words, working-class participation increased by around 10 percentage points, middle-class par-ticipation by around 18 percentage points. Figures from the Office for National Statistics covering a longer time period tell a similar story: between 1960 and 2001, participation among those from the manual social classes increased from 4 to 19 per cent while among the non-manual classes it rose from 27 to 50 per cent (Summerfield and Gill 2005). The middle classes are clearly the main beneficiaries of the growth in the university sector.

The picture in Scotland is slightly different. In Scotland, due to a greater overall tendency to progress to higher education, absolute levels of participa-tion among members of the working classes are higher than in England and Wales, but in relative terms class-based inequalities are somewhat *more* pro-nounced (Iannelli 2007). Greater opportunities to participate at the sub-degree level in Scotland has helped stimulate demand for higher education but has also resulted in a tendency for working-class students to study vocational subjects. Indeed, while the further education sector has provided opportunities for less advantaged students, Osborne and McLaurin have argued that although 'these institutions are creating greater opportunity, particularly for those from traditional non-participant groups, there are also dangers that the articulation arrangements themselves lead to a funnelling of certain types of students into one particular type of institution' (2006: 154–5).

The persistence and growth of class-based inequalities in access to higher education during a period in which the supply of places had increased can be partly explained by the underlying growth in income inequality in a num-ber of advanced societies. In the USA, it has been argued that increasing income inequality (as measured by the Gini coefficient) has led to a 'greater dispersion of educational outcomes . . . primarily because those at the bot-tom of the educational distribution fall further from the mean' (Haveman and Wilson 2007: 32). In other words, growing economic inequality has helped polarize outcomes in secondary education which has knock-on effects on access to university.

While absolute levels of participation in higher education have increased sharply for both males and females, women have been the greater beneficiar-ies. In 1970/71, men outnumbered women by around 2:1, by 2004/05, 57 per cent of participants in higher education were female (Figure 2.1). The watershed was reached in the early 1990s in Scotland and in the mid-1990s in England and Wales (Iannelli 2007) with most of the OECD showing simi-lar trends. By the late 1990s, women comprised the majority of first-time university entrants in 10 out of 13 OECD countries (Skilbeck 2000).

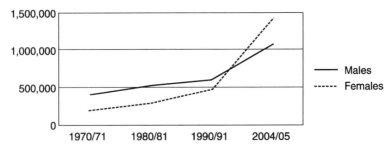

Figure 2.1 Students in higher education, by gender, 1970/71–2004/05, in the UK
Source: Self and Zealey (2007).

The picture for ethnic minority groups is somewhat complex. Despite evidence suggesting that applicants from ethnic minorities are less likely to be offered places in some institutions (Shiner and Modood 2002), many ethnic groups are actually over-represented in higher education compared to their representation in their overall age group (Gilchrist et al. 2003; Connor et al. 2004; Allen and Ainley 2007) and several minority ethnic groups are more likely to obtain degrees (National Statistics 2008). The important issue relates to stratification between institutions and subject areas, by ethnic origin and by gender (Gilchrist et al. 2003). First of all, minority ethnic groups, especially Black African and Afro-Caribbeans, are concentrated in the less prestigious institutions (Connor et al. 2004; Modood 2006; Allen and Ainley 2007). Labour MP David Lammy (*Guardian* 2004a) points out that while black people account for around 5 per cent of the population, they account for less than 0.7 per cent of Cambridge undergraduates. Allen and Ainley make a similar point: 'London Metropolitan University . . . has more black and minority ethnic students than the top twenty "Russell Group" of elite universities put together' (2007: 35). However, it is misleading to portray the experiences of minority ethnic groups as uniform: some minorities fare better than others. Those of Chinese and Indian origin are over-represented on degree courses, for example, while Pakistanis and Bangladeshis are under-represented. Gender also has a cross-cutting effect: in some poorly represented minority groups girls are more likely to access higher education, mainly on account of superior performance at school (Gilchrist et al. 2003; National Statistics 2008).

With strong differentials in levels of attainment between schools serving different neighbourhoods, the chances of participating in higher education vary significantly within any city. The organization and ethos of individual schools can affect patterns of attainment which in turn influence participation rates, although to an extent apparent school effects can be reduced to the impact of concentrated socio-economic advantage and disadvantage. In non-urban areas, schools tend to contain a greater social mix and therefore school-level variation is much weaker. Taking Glasgow as an example of an urban area (Figure 2.2), in the state sector, Notre Dame and Hyndland

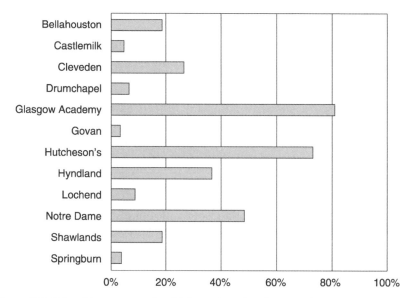

Figure 2.2 School-leavers entering higher education from a selection of Glasgow schools, 2004

Source: Scotland on Sunday (2005). Private school figures kindly provided by the Scottish Government Analytic Services Unit.

schools are both located in the affluent West End of the city and in 2004 sent 48 and 36 per cent of pupils, respectively, directly to higher education. At the other end of the scale, Springburn and Govan, both located in areas of multiple deprivation, sent just 3 per cent to higher education. Two schools shown in Figure 2.2 are private schools: Glasgow Academy and Hutcheson's Grammar. From the former, 82 per cent progressed directly to higher education as did 73 per cent from the latter. Yet these figures are probably an under-estimate. None of the young people from the private schools moved directly to employment or training and with a relatively high proportion having no known destination (11 per cent from Glasgow Academy and 19 per cent from Hutcheson's Grammar), it is likely that some of those unaccounted for will have entered higher education while others might have planned gap years. With relatively high levels of deprivation, in a national context, Glasgow might somewhat atypical, but the figures do show a pattern that is repeated across the country – at one extreme, schools where virtually no one progresses to higher education while at the other extreme there are schools (virtually all private) where the vast majority do progress.

Figures relating to the overall distribution of places in higher education, either geographically or between members of different social classes, genders or ethnic groups provide a vivid picture of persistent inequality. At the same time, the magnitude of the situation can only be appreciated by building in the patterns of horizontal stratification that describe inequalities in the distribution of entrants between institutions and subject areas. It is misleading to talk simply of access to higher education without highlighting the extent to which some groups of entrants access elite institutions or high status courses while others study in less advantaged contexts, entering an understaffed and poorly funded ghetto sector (Field 2004; Osborne and McLaurin 2006).

As key gatekeepers, university admission officers have occupied the firing line: seen by some politicians as frustrating their plans to create a more socially just pattern of entry, and accused by upper middle-class parents as engaged in a process of social engineering whereby highly qualified applicants from private schools are turned away to create space for less well qualified applicants from state schools. Yet as Watson notes, 'genuinely "fair admissions" will involve telling some apparently well qualified students (especially those whose families have spent a lot of disposable income making them so) why they have *not* been selected' (2006: 7, our emphasis). In truth, the universities have been placed in a 'no win' situation. There are now financial implications[1] for institutions that fail to meet targets set by the new Office of Fair Access for recruiting students from less advantaged families. On the other hand, if they accept applicants whom they feel might struggle academically and leave without completing their courses, they can be penalized financially for having high drop-out rates.

The most obvious dimension of horizontal stratification relates to institution hierarchies and to the ways in which students from different social classes are allocated to institutions that reflect their own socio-economic positions. Institutions of higher education organize themselves in ways that help establish and maintain reputations and even form exclusive 'clubs' to signal their position and status and to engage in exclusionary tactics in attempts to secure political and financial advantage. Hence the Russell Group of the 20 major research-led universities regard themselves as occupying the apex of the hierarchy both in terms of status and research income (within the Russell Group, Oxford and Cambridge are regarded as a super-elite). Below the Russell Group in terms of status (and in terms of age), the 1994 group is comprised of 19 of the smaller and more recently established research-led institutions (universities such as Essex, Warwick and York). A differentiation also tends to be made between the pre-1992 universities and the post-1992 universities (mainly consisting of the former polytechnics). At the bottom of the status hierarchy are the colleges of further and higher education that award some degrees as well as some sub-degree qualifications.

There is a clear correspondence between the social class of students and the institutions they attend, and this association is a continual source of political irritation. Students from the upper middle classes (especially those who have been educated privately who account for 39 per cent of the intake of the 'top 13' universities, but just 7 per cent of the population as a whole (Sutton Trust 2000)) are highly over-represented in a small cluster of Russell Group universities, such as Oxford, Cambridge, St Andrews, Bristol and Durham. In a less privileged position, those from working-class families are highly concentrated in the former polytechnics and the college sector. To put this in context, Oxford, Cambridge, Bristol and Durham all draw more than 85 per cent of students from the middle classes[2] (Figure 2.3). In sharp contrast, Harper Adams, UHI Millennium Institute and Wolverhampton all draw more than 50 per cent of their students from working-class families (Figure 2.4).

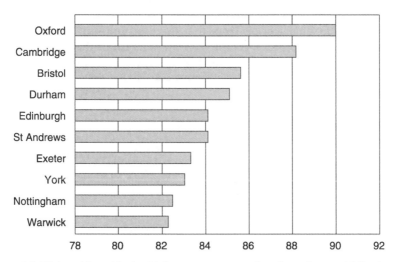

Figure 2.3 Universities with the highest percentage of students from middle-class families

Source: Sunday Times 2008.

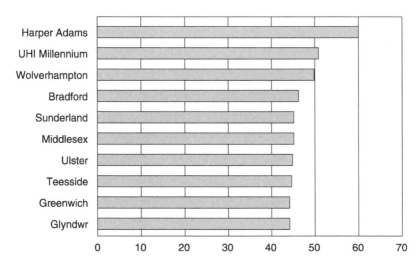

Figure 2.4 Universities with the highest percentage of students from working-class families

Source: Sunday Times 2008.

In an attempt to incentivize the development of wider access strategies, the Office of Fair Access is authorized to allow English institutions to charge 'top-up' fees of up to £3,225 per student[3] so long as they meet access agreements based on benchmark figures for recruitment from working-class families, state schools or colleges and low participation neighbourhoods. These benchmarks and the achievements of institutions are published by the Higher Education Statistics Agency (HESA) on an annual basis. Statistics on admissions from state schools show that some institutions (mainly, but not exclusively) ex-polytechnics, recruit over 98 per cent of their students from state schools while others (mainly members of the Russell Group) recruit less than two-thirds from state schools (Figure 2.5). Given that just 7 per cent of

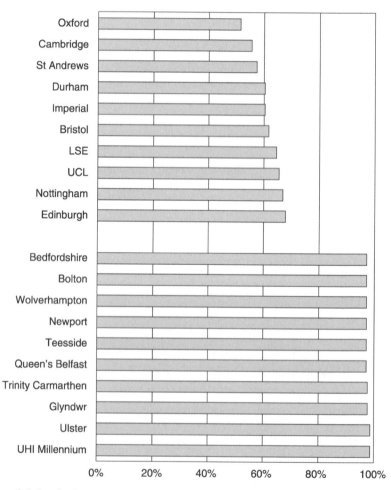

Figure 2.5 Intake from state schools: lowest and highest, 2006

Source: Sunday Times 2008.

pupils are educated outside of the state sector, the targets set by the Office of Fair Access are hardly ambitious. The worst offenders, Oxford and Cambridge, must aim to recruit around 75 per cent of students from the state sector (rather than the 93 per cent that an outsider might think would be required to demonstrate fair access): at present, Oxford recruits just 53.0 per cent and Cambridge 57.6 per cent from the state sector and Oxford's Chancellor recently stated that his university had 'no chance whatsoever of meeting the socio-economic targets set by the agents of government' (*Times Higher* 2008a).

Statistics on recruitment of students from low participation neighbour-hoods (defined as neighbourhoods where participation rates are less than two-thirds of the UK average) also highlight the severity of horizontal stratifi-cation. At one extreme, the University of Sunderland recruits 35 per cent of its students from low participation neighbourhoods while Oxford, Cambridge and Bristol recruit around 5 per cent (HESA 2007a). Again, the benchmarks can be met without undermining established patterns of stratification: Oxford, for example, has a target of 8.5 per cent. To meet these modest targets, the most socially exclusive institutions have had to put greater effort into recruiting high achieving state-educated pupils while setting higher tar-iffs for the privately educated. This has caused an outcry from patrons of the private sector and led to accusations of social engineering and injustice in the treatment of 'bright' young people who 'worked hard' (or whose parents paid well) to achieve top grades. Nevertheless, there is evidence of an increase in the recruitment of students from low participation neighbour-hoods. The Sutton Trust (2005b) has shown that between 1997/98 and 2002/03 there was a 49 per cent increase in the number of entrants to what they refer to as the 'leading 13' universities by young people from low participation neighbourhoods (a seemingly large increase, but one which, relating to a small baseline, has led to little real change).

Another important dimension of horizontal stratification relates to subject areas and is manifest most strongly in the binary division between vocational and non-vocational subjects. With a few high prestige exceptions in areas such as law and medicine, vocational subjects were once uncommon within the university sector and tended to be located in colleges and polytechnics where they could be studied at sub-degree level. Indeed, a substantial part of the growth of higher education has resulted from the establishment of degree entry in a range of areas that once either required diplomas or simply sought evidence of a good general education. Working-class students have always been more likely to study vocational subjects and subjects that have clear career links rather than general academic subjects, especially where these subjects are unfamiliar or perceived as being 'posh'. Subjects like busi-ness and management, engineering and teaching have traditionally appealed to working-class students, and the new degree subjects in areas such as nurs-ing, information systems and building surveying have proved popular.

Figures from the central clearing house for university entry (UCAS) show very clear differences in patterns of application to various subject areas that are linked to the social class of parents of aspiring students (Figure 2.6). With relatively few applications from working-class students, the middle classes dominate applications in all subject areas. However, in high prestige subjects applicants are overwhelmingly drawn from the middle classes. In medicine and dentistry, for example, more than seven in ten applicants were from the managerial and professional classes compared to just one in ten from the routine and semi-routine classes. With subjects like nursing and physiotherapy requiring lower entry qualifications and being offered mainly in the new universities, working-class students can regard this area as more accessible (and perhaps more class-appropriate). As such, subjects allied to medicine (which includes nursing) attracts the largest number of working-class students: in 2006, 26 per cent of students applying for subjects in this cluster came from the routine and semi-routine classes (compared to 46 per cent from the managerial and professional classes).

Horizontal stratification between subjects that predominantly attract particular genders and minority ethnic groups are also significant. In 2004/05, four subject areas accounted for just over half the female students in the UK: subjects allied to medicine, education, business and administrative studies and social studies. Males tended not to cluster quite so tightly within a restricted range of subject areas, although 45 per cent of male students studied business and administrative studies, engineering and technology, computer science and social studies (Self and Zealey 2007). Here we must also note that despite a predominance of female over male undergraduates, females are over-represented in less prestigious subject areas (such as subjects allied to medicine). Similar patterns of stratification by subject apply to minority ethnic groups, partly, but not entirely, as a result of their concentration in new universities. Subjects like pharmacy and business, for

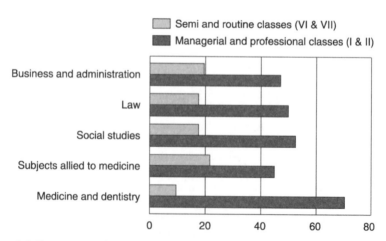

Figure 2.6 Percentage of upper- and lower-class applicants applying for university courses in a selection of subjects

Source: Derived from UCAS statistics on applications, 2007.

example, have attracted relatively large numbers of minority ethnic applicants (Gilchrist et al. 2003; National Statistics 2008).

Explaining inequality of access

The rapid growth in levels of participation in higher education occurring over the past couple of decades has parallels in most advanced nations. There are several reasons for growth. The first relates to employment trends and is linked to globalization and the location of high skill, high-value labour in the dominant economic regions. With manufacture and many routine services located in developing countries, western labour markets have polarized with a growth in professional, technical and managerial positions at one end of the scale and the maintenance of a strong basic service sector at the other end (Beck 2000; Furlong and Kelly 2005). These changes have led to a shift in the balance of opportunities which, together with the development of new educational routes, have encouraged young people to embark on courses of higher education that are seen as facilitating access to the more desirable sectors of the labour market. The government has also promoted the expansion of higher education by setting a target of 50 per cent of 18–30 year olds entering by 2010,[4] motivated by the belief that a more educated workforce would stimulate economic growth and lead to returns to the exchequer through additional tax revenue. In the words of David Blunkett, the Secretary of State for Education and Employment from 1997 to 2001, economic prosperity in the nineteenth century rested on the 'power of the machine' while success in the modern world increasingly rests on 'intellectual capital' (DfEE 1997: 2).

A second important factor has been the increase in the number of school-leavers who are qualified to enter higher education (OECD 2007). This occurred partly as a result of labour market changes which led to a significant decrease in the availability of jobs for minimum-aged leavers. With a reduced 'pull' from the labour market and with many young people sceptical about the value of government-supported work-based training schemes, remaining at school became a more attractive option, even for some of those who had a preference for rapid labour market entry (Raffe and Willms 1989). A third factor relates to cultural change, expressed on the one hand by a weakening of visible class-based divisions in the secondary school (Biggart and Furlong 1996) and on the other by more educated parents who encourage their children to consider extended education (Burnhill 1984; Croxford et al. 2006).

In the context of social justice, the key question relates to how socio-economic divisions in access to higher education can be maintained (even strengthened) during a period of rapid expansion. At the very heart of the issue of fair access is the problem of qualifications and advantages enjoyed by the middle classes, especially those with the ability to afford private education. For under-represented groups, the main barrier to accessing higher education stems from having inferior qualifications. Therefore, the first and most significant step to social justice in higher education is about improving the quality of primary and secondary education, especially for those groups who are under-performing. But schools do not operate in a vacuum; patterns of parental encouragement and cultural capital represent a *habitus* (Bourdieu 1977) that has an important bearing on school experiences and perform-ance. In the UK and many other countries, schooling is a stratified process. The existence of geographic catchment areas mean that many schools are dominated by members of particular social classes and aspirations in working-class schools can be restricted. This process is reinforced by the existence of strong private and grant maintained sectors, while the use of academic and vocational streams also serves to reinforce socio-economic divisions (Ford 1969; Ball 1981). As Watson observes, equalization is not achieved 'by separating sheep from goats, whether or not the pens are labelled "academic" and "vocational" or "public" and "private" ' (2006: 8).

With educational qualifications used as currency to purchase access to higher education, admissions policies can maintain a veneer of fairness based on the perceived link between merit and performance. The failure by some groups to make significant inroads to higher education can then be blamed on a lack of individual effort, ability or aspirations with suggestions to reduce entry tariffs to disadvantaged groups met with the charge that standards are being eroded. In this respect, politicians have tended to be half-hearted in their efforts to achieve more socially just access policies and have been somewhat too eager to lay the blame at the door of the universities who are portrayed as operating unfair access and selection policies. Admis-sions policies and the presumed prejudices of middle-class admissions officers can make good press and are an easy target for politicians. A few years ago Gordon Brown publicly criticized Oxford University for rejecting a state school student, Laura Spence, who despite having straight As at A level, was refused a place to study medicine. In their defence, admissions officers point out that restrictions on places and high levels of demand for some courses mean that they frequently have to choose between candidates who are equally well qualified and in these instances are forced to look beyond qualifications.

At the same time, there is evidence showing that even when they obtain the highest grades, young people from working-class families are disadvan-taged in the selection process. This is especially true in the case of courses, like medicine, which have a high middle-class demand (Thomas et al. 2005). Socially just admissions policies have to take account of advantages and dis-advantages associated with the family as well as those encountered during the process of schooling which justify positive discrimination: a policy few politicians are willing to whole-heartedly endorse and only a small number of brave vice-chancellors are prepared to sanction. Furthermore, approaches that focus on entrance qualifications and overt decision-making processes among committed applicants fall short of the mark. In general, it is the middle-class student who embarks on a process of 'rational' decision-making, although among all potential students decisions are frequently based on 'hunches, feelings or emotions' (Gewirtz et al. 1993, quoted in Hutchings 2003: 97). Hutchings argues that, for most young people, entry to higher education rarely involves an identifiable 'moment of decision' (2003: 97); some will always have seen university entry as part of a process of natural educational progression while others never come to entertain the idea. Leathwood argues that for many young people from working-class families, the risks associated with higher education are higher and, as such, non-participation could be considered to be a 'rational response to an unfair and unequal system (2006: 19). The risks she regards as being particularly salient include financial risks as well as the risk of failure and threats to class-based identity.

A lack of understanding of working-class culture and a poor ability to 'read' the motives and commitment of non-traditional students may underpin some unjust decisions about admissions, especially when an interview plays a part in the selection process.[5] Poor levels of engagement with an interviewer and a lack of confidence to develop an argument can be interpreted as reflecting a lack of ability, as can an ignorance of 'high-brow' culture. More fundamentally, admissions officers may fail to appreciate that a potential student from a working-class family who attended a state school and who presents with low grade A levels or Highers is in many ways the academic equivalent to a middle-class student with good A levels who has benefitted from a private education. While institutions may look sympathetically at the grades achieved by a working-class applicant, there is often a genuine (and misplaced) concern that such students are less able and may struggle to cope with their courses. These concerns are expressed candidly in relation to students with qualifications such as HNCs and HNDs[6] which are delivered in further education colleges but designed to allow progression to higher education. While new universities are happy to admit people with these qualifications, and may even exempt them from the first or second year of study, the older universities tend to look less favourably on these candidates (Scottish Funding Council 2007).

To an extent, universities fear the unknown and those institutions that have a strong upper middle-class ethos and which recruit heavily from the private schools can be concerned that working-class students may 'pollute the pristine and pure university environment' (Leadiwood and O'Connell 2003: 599). Here Tysome (2002) quotes the Chief Executive of the Council for Education and Industry referring to non-traditional students as the 'unwashed' and notes fears that working-class students lack the soft skills to co-exist with their middle-class peers.

The suspicion of different cultures is mutual and can be regarded as a key process through which separations between the worlds inhabited by different classes are maintained. These cultural differences are effectively illustrated through interviews with 'qualified but disadvantaged' young people who participated in a recent longitudinal study conducted in the West of Scotland (Forsyth and Furlong 2000, 2003; Furlong and Cartmel 2005). (Full details of the study, referred to here and in subsequent chapters as the West of Scotland study, are contained in the Appendix.) Voicing these cultural suspicions from a working-class perspective, one young woman who partici- pated in the West of Scotland study expressed her alienation from her middle-class peers:

> They all speak a certain way and you are not impressive any more, but then you . . . are poorer. I did not feel working class until I went to uni . . . and now I feel incredibly working class and I feel like a wee socialist that stands up for what she believes in.
>
> (Heather)

Another student who was invited to an interview at Cambridge University said that she had real difficulty relating to any of the other applicants that she met at an open day on account of their social backgrounds, as she put it, 'I could hardly make out what they were saying, never mind talk to them' (Rachel).

An important but frequently overlooked asset affecting access to higher education is knowledge. Here those from families or from schools who have had extensive contact with universities have a distinct advantage and are able to draw on information about opportunities that other groups lack (Thomas 2001). First generation applicants from schools that send few pupils on to university can find it difficult to choose between institutions and courses and the process of choice can be perceived as complex (Connor et al. 1999). The terminology can be unfamiliar and potential students are left bewildered by the numerous choices that face them and unaware of the range of possible options. In this context it has been argued that the development of a com- plex market for education changes the 'rules of engagement' and strength- ens the position of the middle classes (Brown 1995: 43). Indeed, Croxford and Raffe argue that the marketization of higher education can be seen as a 'new mechanism of social closure' (2005: 2) in which the middle classes are well placed to take advantage of opportunities.

Advice provided by teachers and the careers service can be perceived as superficial and as inadequate for those who have little idea about institutions of higher education, course options or future careers (Thomas et al. 2002). Young people from families where there is no previous experience of higher education often lack a basic knowledge of universities, of subjects and of how to apply or how to fund their studies (Forsyth and Furlong 2000):

> I didn't really get much guidance about what to apply for at university and I didn't have a clue what I wanted to study, so I applied for engin- eering courses because I've done physics. After submitting my applica- tion, I suddenly thought 'Oh, my God, I really don't want to do that at all, it's going to be so boring' so I changed the application.
>
> (Jessie)

Several young people suggested that teachers and careers officers should be more proactive in motivating potential students. In schools serving deprived areas, pupils frequently felt that the teachers placed an emphasis on finding jobs rather than on higher education: according to one young woman:

> I honestly think the teachers have to make some sort of effort within the schools, something to inspire confidence. But, see, I'm sure they just don't know what they were doing, you know what I mean. See, if somebody was to say 'you are quite good at that', listen, 'he is good at this' and 'she is good at that', and 'why don't you try this?' or something like that. A lot of people just don't think they can go to university, they just don't think.
>
> (Rachel)

Interviews with young people in the West of Scotland frequently illustrated a culturally framed communication gap and pointed towards the existence of class-based stereotypes among teachers and careers advisers who, from the perspective of young people, were seen as undermining their plans and attempting to 'cool out' their aspirations. At the same time, there was evidence of mutual support systems through which young people who aspired to university or college helped support and encourage each other and found a sense of belonging in a school context where they were somewhat atypical:

> Well, definitely in my situation, I was very lucky, although I went to what is considered quite a bad school. Within the school there was a definite network of people that were all, who was wanting to go on to further education, and it was not a problem. I think there needs to be some kind of support to get those people together to be a group because it meant that within the system you had a kind of place you belonged.
>
> (Heather)

It was also clear that some young people faced pressure from friends and family not to pursue higher education and a strong counterbalance was sometime necessary to help them maintain aspirations. One young woman who decided not to go on to higher education recollected that whenever the subject of university came up, her mother and father would say 'just think of the debt you'll get into' (Lucy) while a young woman faced pressure from her boyfriend who told her that if she remained in education she would 'turn into a freak' (Libby). Several young people were warned about the risk in following higher educational pathways. As one young man who decided not to go to university told us:

> My Dad said it a few times, that he had heard stories about people going to college and going to university and getting degrees and ending up with nothing at the end of it. I thought about that.
>
> (Glen)

In the main, though, these qualified but disadvantaged young people thought that their families had been supportive, even when they were initially taken aback by the decision or had a negative view about certain professions. Parents were often proud that their child had enjoyed a successful educational career and were willing to provide whatever help they could even when this involved severe family hardship:

> I think they were quite shocked that I wanted to go to uni, actually because none of my family had really been to university or like into any kind of further education apart from one uncle. But I think they were quite pleased, hoping me to do quite well. They were quite encouraging, I think they just wanted me to move out of the house but, yeah, they were actually quite good.
>
> (Jane)

Student subjectivity clearly plays a major role in patterns of access and the aspirations and expectations of working-class students are frequently low. Aspirations are important and students can gain motivation from being able to make linkages between their studies and future occupational engagement. It is not necessary to have fixed occupational aspirations (and many students have few ideas about what they might do after completing their education), but it is useful if young people can appreciate the broad relevance of their level of study for future employment. Here the selection of courses and applications for entry, and often the effort put into school work, may be linked to desired future lifestyle packages in which 'possible futures' (Markus and Nurius 1986) are linked to educational pathways. Ideas about the linkages between qualifications and lifestyle can be as important as specific occupational goals.

> Well, I think it is very important to me because it means I can get the chance to do something, like, I mean, none of my family have got, like, degrees or anything. So it means that I have got the chance to do something that none of them have done and it gives me a chance, like, maybe see a bit of the world depending on what I decide to do.
>
> (Maureen)

In the context of aspirations, Reay (2005) argues that for young people from working-class families, educational decisions are often framed by the need to secure an identity underpinned by a class-based 'authenticity'. For Reay, the participation of working-class students is not about casting aside a working-class identity but is driven by a desire to accommodate their new experiences within a framework that respects their working-class roots. As Reay puts it, 'for the working class student authenticity most often meant being able to hold onto a self rooted in a working class past' (2005: 7). From the point of view of those who participated in the West of Scotland survey, the need to frame biographies in the context of a class-based authenticity was an important part of a risk management strategy within contexts that could be interpreted as strange and even threatening (see also Macrae and Maguire 2002).

Conclusion

Despite the huge increase in participation in higher education occurring in the UK and most other advanced countries in the past four decades, the middle classes have been the main beneficiaries. Indeed, while there has been an overall increase in the numbers of working-class students in higher education, their relative gains have been negligible (even non-existent). However, if we scratch the surface, the picture looks worse. Not only are the working classes in a poor position when it comes to access, patterns of horizontal stratification mean that they are overwhelmingly concentrated in the new universities and, even when they do access the elite universities, they tend to be excluded from the more prestigious subjects.

In this chapter we have provided vivid evidence relating to the stratification of opportunities in higher education. Like other commentators, our position is that the roots of access inequality stretch far back into the years of primary and secondary education which results in a situation where in some schools very few young people emerge with the qualifications that allow progress to university while in others (mainly private) virtually everyone is able to progress. Success at school is crucial as most 'qualified but disadvantaged' young people do progress directly to higher education or have a desire to do so and their parents tend to be supportive of their decisions (Forsyth and Furlong 2003).

While universities' admissions policies can make a difference, especially if a positive discrimination strategy is employed, reform of admissions procedures is not sufficient to bring about significant change. In many ways the older universities have an image problem, primarily of their own making, that has exclusionary consequences. In seeking to present themselves as elite institutions that have a reputation for producing past and future leaders, they can alienate working-class and minority ethnic students who lack the confidence (arrogance?) to pigeon-hole themselves as part of an elite (which may be associated with a white upper class). Potential students themselves make choices that reinforce existing systems of stratification, but they do not act in a vacuum. There is often a tension between identities framed within a working-class tradition and the middle-class identities projected by the older universities which, as Reay (2007) has argued, must be resolved in ways that permit the retention of a class-based authenticity. Similarly, it has been argued (Ball et al. 2002) that potential students from minority ethnic groups can be concerned about fitting into older universities where they will be in a small minority.

In subsequent chapters we will look more closely at the tensions between class-based identities and university experience. But the main message to take forward from this chapter is that the establishment of a socially just system requires radical changes that go far beyond revising admissions policies.

3

Reinforcing inequality through funding policies

Policy should not be based on an *assumption* that parents will support their children. Such an assumption may, at a stretch, have been valid for an elite system of higher education, regarded as a luxury good for middle-class families; it is invalid for mass higher education as an investment good, and totally inapplicable to a policy of expanding access to groups with no previous experience of higher education.

(Barr 2001: 205, original emphasis)

Introduction

The expansion of higher education presents a dilemma for governments. At a time when a small fraction of an age cohort entered higher education, the costs to central government of absorbing tuition fees and even of contributing towards living costs caused few concerns even to the most prudent finance ministers. As participation increased, governments became more reluctant to pass the costs of education in its entirety to the (individual or corporate) taxpayer. While recognizing the public benefits of a system of mass higher education, in many countries governments have increasingly taken the view that individual beneficiaries and their families should bear a significant proportion of the costs.

In this context there has been a tendency to try and portray education as a consumer product that individual participants are expected to finance in anticipation of personal economic advantage secured on the basis of advanced credentials. The principled objection to fees on the grounds of social justice is no longer as evident as it was in the recent past. At the same time, governments have been acutely aware of the issue of affordability and of the potential for fee regimes to conflict with and subvert wider access policies.

There is clear evidence from all of the developed countries that those from the wealthiest families are most likely to attend university and are strongly over-represented in the most prestigious universities (see Chapter 2). In countries where universities charge variable fees, such as the USA, students from the wealthiest families are concentrated in high-cost institutions while poor students are over-represented in community colleges (McPherson and Schapiro 1999; Goldhaber and Peri 2007). Yet institutional stratification occurs in most countries, irrespective of fee regimes. Indeed, the correlation between family wealth and university recruitment is not in itself proof that the cost of a university education represents a significant barrier to access. In all developed countries there are mechanisms to help support students from less-advantaged families, often in the form of means-tested grants, fee waivers or scholarships provided by universities. One of the issues that can obscure the relationship between wealth and recruitment relates to a process of self-selection. Students from poorer families are less likely to apply to university than their more affluent peers, and while this might reflect affordability, it is also likely to involve poorer levels of attainment during the school years, a lack of knowledge about opportunities as well as differential aspirations. Researchers have yet to fully disentangle these issues or isolate the impact of financial resources on patterns of access to higher education.

In this chapter we look at the compatibility between funding regimes and the equal opportunities agenda. We examine the ways in which the choices made by young people from working-class families are affected by cost, and look at the effectiveness of a range of mechanisms which have been put in place in an attempt to prevent financial deterrence. With attitudes towards money and debt varying between social groups, we explore their impact on educational choices. Highlighting the illusion of choice created by the marketization of education, we suggest that funding regimes help draw attention away from the entrenchment of traditional forms of inequality.

Social justice and funding policies

If we are concerned to develop a socially just system of higher education, where all who are capable of benefitting are able to do so irrespective of family income or wealth, how should it be funded? Obviously many potential students would be unable to afford the full economic costs of their tuition or the expense of removing themselves from the full-time labour market for several years while they focus on their studies. Either the state must bear these costs, in anticipation of eventual returns via tax on future earnings and spending, or a means must be found of subsidizing at least a proportion of the cost through grants or by backing a system of loans to students or their families.

With the emergence of a mass system of higher education, funding issues have become more contentious, as the Blair government discovered when it tried to get parliamentary approval for its Higher Education Bill in 2004.[1] The importance of developing a funding regime that does not discourage working-class students from attending university enjoyed cross-party support, but even within the government benches there were serious divisions as to whether the proposals being considered were socially just or whether they would deter potential students from poorer families. Supporters of the bill argued that the changes provide more support for those from low income families and less for the sons and daughters of high earners who will be ineligible for bursaries and will only be entitled to 75 per cent of the maximum student loan. Those opposed regarded the policies as representing a further barrier to working-class participation.

If ministers were to seek guidance through observing the practice of foreign governments, they would have remained confused as to the best way forward. Among countries with mass systems of higher education, there are huge variations in practice with many governments still exploring ways of funding a modern system of higher education. Practice covers the full spectrum ranging from a market-based model where governments provide minimal funds to institutions or individual students, to a fully developed model of socialized delivery in which the state accepts responsibility for funding higher education institutions as well as covering a proportion of the costs of those who attend them (Figure 3.1). The USA comes close to the market-based typology while the Scandinavian countries are closer to the social model. The UK falls towards the centre of the model, with a tendency for new policies to increasingly lean towards market-based approaches. Despite strong differences, across the spectrum, governments frequently feel able to justify their approaches in terms of social justice.

Before exploring the philosophical underpinnings of debates around social justice and funding regimes, it is worth describing some of the variations in the practice of a few countries in a little more detail so as to be aware of existing practice in a broad context and to highlight associated difficulties.

In the USA, education is a federal responsibility, but few states have accepted a major responsibility for funding higher education and there has never been a strong tradition of providing free access to higher education or of covering the living costs of students. Around half of all higher education

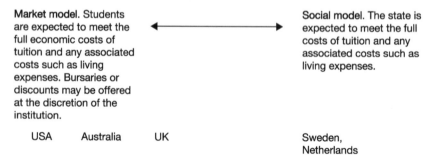

Figure 3.1 Typologies of funding regime

institutions are private and fees in both public and private sectors tend to be determined by the institutions themselves. Tuition fees cover around 41 per cent of the income of private institutions and 27 per cent of public institutions (Barr 2001). Student support comes from a variety of sources including parental contributions, part-time employment, federal and state loans as well as privately secured loans and college bursaries and, for students from low income families federally funded, non-repayable, grants[2] (Barr 2001; Usher 2005). It is misleading to speak of a US 'system' (Barr 2001; Stone 2009) as provision is diverse and student experiences hugely varied. With a large majority of young people graduating from high school and thus being eligible to progress to higher education,[3] rates of participation are very high with more than six in ten experiencing higher education (OECD 2004). Provision tends to be very flexible with students often able to determine levels of participation and speed of progression, resulting in a high propor-tion of mature students. There is also some articulation between local com-munity colleges and institutions of higher education which (theoretically) allows students to progress from college to university (Bonham 2005).[4] Yet in the USA this mass participation, flexible 'system' also remains powerfully stratified. Community colleges, which are a relatively low cost option, are popular with students from low income families (McPherson and Schapiro 1999; Goldhaber and Peri 2007) while 'Ivy League' institutions, like Harvard and Yale, are linked strongly to the social elite. While the Ivy League uni-versities are keen to make the public aware that they set some funds aside to provide bursaries for students unable to meet their fees,[5] the overwhelming majority of students are from the upper middle classes[6] with many of the elite institutions having a tradition of recruiting disproportionate numbers of WASPs (White Anglo-Saxon Protestants) and evidence that some have actively discriminated against black, Jewish and female applicants (Karabel 2005). In the USA, social class has a clear impact on college attendance and graduation rates with students whose parents are in the top income quartile being four times more likely to graduate than ones from the lowest income quartile (Haveman and Wilson 2007).

While in the region of six in ten full-time undergraduates in the USA receive some means-tested financial assistance, overall levels of debt are high with strong variations between graduates of public and private universities, largely due to differential fees.[7] Tuition fees represent a significant propor-tion of overall debt, averaging $10,000 per year in low-cost state universities compared to $25,000 per year in high-cost private universities (Education in the USA 2007). Yale, for example, charges a fee of $27,300 a year for its forestry course, but, with living costs and other associated fees the university suggests potential students budget for $46,565 per anum (Yale School of Forestry and Environmental Studies 1997). These significant variations in cost mean that students frequently select courses on the basis of afford-ability, taking account of available support such as bursaries (Independent Committee of Inquiry into Student Finance 1999).

Like the US 'system', Australian higher education also involves high levels of participation with around 77 per cent enrolling in higher education (OECD 2004). Although the state funds institutions of higher education, fees, which vary according to courses taken, are payable by students. Those taking courses like law, where economic returns to the student are high, pay the vast majority of the costs of the course. Subjects linked to poorer individual returns but with a high national value, such as agriculture, attract far lower fees. Students are eligible for low interest, means-tested loans to cover the cost of tuition but are not offered any help to cover living costs which tend to be paid for by a combination of parental contribution, income from part-time work and private loan. It has been argued that the introduction of an income-contingent charging system has not had an impact on the participation rates of low income groups (Chapman and Ryan 2002).

Although fees do not vary by institution in Australia, and while there is no evidence suggesting that the imposition of fees has deterred less advantaged students, there are a number of processes through which stratification occurs and levels of participation among those from low-income groups are poor (Independent Committee of Inquiry into Student Finance 1999). First, the lack of state support for living costs and the need for parents to contribute, but also substantial discounts (25 per cent) available to those who pay fees upfront effectively mean that students from poorer families pay significantly more for their education. Second, the existence of differential fees and their impact on selection for the most prestigious courses, such as law, where students pay around 80 per cent of cost. Third, perceptions of an institutional hierarchy among students and their parents in which some universities are clearly viewed as more elitist than others (reinforced by use of terms such as the 'Group of Eight' to refer to the leading universities). Fourth, the existence of a strong TAFE (Technical and Further Education) sector offering vocational qualifications and attracting many working-class students.

The funding situation in Sweden is very different with the system following more of a social rather than a market-based approach. The government provides funding for all higher educational institutions and students are not required to pay any tuition fees. The government also makes a major contribution towards students' living costs by providing a grant that covers around 28 per cent of the typical students' living costs and issuing heavily subsidized loans to cover the remainder of their maintenance. While loans are means-tested, they take account of the income of the students themselves with no consideration being made of parental income or wealth (Barr 2001). Graduates must repay their loans at a rate of 4 per cent of income per year once they have completed their studies, but at the age of 65 any remaining debt will be cancelled. The low rate of repayment combined with relatively lengthy courses means that many graduates will eventually have their debt written off, leading Barr to suggest that it can actually be regarded as a form of graduate tax.[8] Other Scandinavian countries, as well as the Netherlands, have adopted broadly similar approaches to student funding usually involving free tuition and combining a subsidized loan with a grant. Like the USA and Australia, the Scandinavian countries are also high participation countries with around 75 per cent participating in Sweden and 71 per cent in Finland (OECD 2004).

With everyone having access to packages of funding to cover living costs and with no deterrent effect from fees, the social model should be linked to a strongly egalitarian system of higher education. Indeed, Sweden, Finland and the Netherlands have been regarded as providing the most affordable systems (Shah 2006). However, in reality, things are a little more complex. First, as in other countries, the experience of compulsory education is stratified with working-class pupils and those from minorities often lacking the qualifications to progress to the most prestigious courses or institutions (Berggren 2008). Second, there is evidence of a poverty of ambition reflected in a lack of interest in higher education among the lower working classes: the Finnish psychologist Jari-Erik Nurmi has written extensively about the impact of personal goals on educational outcomes (Nurmi et al. 2002, 2003). In the Scandinavian countries there is a clear stratification in the provision of higher education: some institutions are clearly seen as more prestigious than others and there are often parallel systems. In Finland, for example, there is a division between the university and polytechnic sectors and, despite a commitment to social justice, an extremely strong link between parental educational experience and access to higher education (Parjanen and Tuomi 2003).

With significant differences emerging between Scotland, England and Wales and Northern Ireland, it is no longer possible to speak of a UK system, but in broad terms the UK can be said to occupy a centre ground between the market and social models. It is a hybrid system in which fees are either subsidized for all (as in England and Wales) or waived for the majority of undergraduates (as in Scotland). Provision is made for a means-tested contribution towards living costs through subsidized loans, although most students will need to supplement their loan through parental contributions, part-time jobs and private loans, especially if they study away from home. In a bid to strengthen economic independence, universities in England and Wales, virtually all of which are public institutions, have recently been granted the power to introduce 'differential' fees of up to £3,225 per year. In practice, virtually all took advantage of the changes by charging the maximum. Hence the addition has become a 'top-up fee' rather than a 'differential' fee. In return for being allowed to increase fees, universities were required to offer bursaries (typically between £1,000 and £2,000 per year, with a small number offering £3,000 or more) for the poorest students and to begin to implement fairer access policies. It is too early to assess the impact of these changes: clearly the introduction of bursaries provides an additional source of funds for some of the poorest students, yet those attending institutions dominated by working-class students have access to less generous provision (*Times Higher* 2008b).

In the UK, as in many other countries, the cost of higher education can deter (Connor et al. 1999; Forsyth and Furlong 2000; Connor et al. 2001;

National Audit Office 2002; Callender 2003; Forsyth and Furlong 2003; Callender and Jackson 2005), but this also leads to situations where potential students explore cost-saving options that result in the purchase of a less than ideal product by those who lack resources or who are reluctant to take on debt (Forsyth and Furlong 2000; Connor et al. 2001; Christie and Munro 2003; Forsyth and Furlong 2003).[9] In other words, costs associated with university are not simply linked to exclusion, but can result in complex forms of stratification among participants.

In many respects it can be misleading to present countries as having uniform approaches towards funding higher education. In most countries there are significant patterns of stratification which result in certain types of institution (usually those considered to form an elite) being located more towards the market model while others (usually sectors catering for 'non-traditional' students) come closer to a social model. Processes of stratification also mean that some of the more prestigious courses (such as medicine or law) are concentrated in the market-based sector while less prestigious and more vocational courses are over-represented in the social sector. Figure 3.2 provides an illustration of some patterns of funding regime stratification in the UK and the USA.

Reflecting on the above examples of funding regimes, it becomes clear that positioning of courses or institutions within contexts that are, in different ways, subject to some market forces, can be regarded as a tool through which class-based segregation is maintained in higher education. Scarce goods, such as prestigious courses at elite universities, are positioned in a way that restrict access, effectively smoothing entry for those with resources and placing barriers in front of those lacking the appropriate resources. The stratification of provision in a way that lubricates processes of social reproduction is fairly ubiquitous in the advanced societies, but tends to be obscured by the provision of 'second rate' alternatives packaged and branded as equivalents.

With these issues in mind, it is important to reflect on the most effective ways to fund a system of higher education that is underpinned by principles

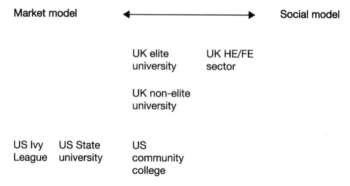

Figure 3.2 Funding regimes and patterns of stratification: the UK and the USA

of social justice and designed to ensure that all young people are able to access a world-class higher education irrespective of their social or economic circumstances.

What's fair?

In the UK, large sections of the public as well as significant numbers of MPs from all political parties hold firmly to the view that education should be free at the point of access. Tuition fees, which are still relatively new in a UK context, are seen by many as a deterrent to entry and as a severe obstacle to those from poorer families, yet there are also arguments in favour of tuition fees. Some of these arguments, as presented by the Scottish Independent Committee of Inquiry into Student Finance (1999), are summarized in Table 3.1.

While the provision of means-tested, non-repayable grants to cover living costs had been seen as central to the provision of equal opportunities between 1962 and 1998, the public have, to an extent, become accustomed to student loans,[10] although many express concerns about levels of student debt and some are concerned that the fear of debt encourages less affluent young people to reject higher education. There are probably two key arguments that have helped persuade the public that students should make a significant contribution to the cost of their education. The first relates to the issue of general affordability in a context where one in two young people will soon be attending higher education. If fees and maintenance grants are met from the public purse, then the burden will be felt by all taxpayers and there are possible repercussions for economic competitiveness. The view that the public at large (especially those who will not benefit from higher education) should not be asked to carry the cost is widespread, a view supported by the economist Nicholas Barr:

> A high-quality mass system cannot be entirely taxpayer funded. Thus public funds have to be supplemented by private funds. This conclusion is not based on ideology, but on the deeply practical reason that large-scale higher education is vital but too expensive to rely entirely on public funding . . . Higher education creates a private benefit: the typical student benefits personally from a degree, through higher earnings, greater job satisfaction, and/or greater enjoyment of leisure. Thus the theory argues unambiguously that some of the costs should be borne by the student.
>
> (Barr 2001: 194–5)

While we are not entirely convinced by the affordability position,[11] the second argument (and the one that has attracted widespread sympathy) is contained in the latter part of the above quote: higher education confers clear benefits on the individual student and therefore the beneficiary should pay. Higher education is often regarded as a personal investment and

Table 3.1 Arguments for and against the payment of tuition fees by students

	Arguments for tuition fees	*Arguments for free higher education*
Financial motives	Tuition fees are an essential element in financing higher education at a time of 'massification' of education and reduced public expenditure.	
Public or private investment	Higher education is a personal as well as a collective investment in which individuals benefit more than society. If higher education is free, all taxpayers have to pay for provision from which only some benefit directly.	Introduction of fees overlooks the fact that investment in higher education is above all a social investment. Higher education is a national priority.
Means of exerting pressure on institutions	Students or their families become consumers in a market situation. Higher education institutions that depend on tuition fees enter into competition with each other, and strive to offer students quality service.	Results, such as better quality education, or competitive institutions, may well be achieved by other means.
Fairness of the system	Without tuition fees, taxpayers in the poorest social groups contribute to investment whose main gains are personal, yet the proportion of students from disadvantaged groups is small.	Fees act as a barrier, or filter, obstructing only students from lower socio-economic groups.
Student motivation to do well	Tuition fees maximize the likelihood of attainment because the individual investment motivates students.	Student motivation can be secured by other means.
Selection of the best students	Only those who are confident of their intellectual ability will opt for higher education if tuition fees are a major element in the decision.	If fees are associated with academic attainment, students from poor social backgrounds are at a disadvantage.

Source: Independent Committee of Inquiry into Student Finance (1999: 40).

therefore the individual should make a contribution. Crudely, why should the factory worker or the shop worker cover the costs of the student lawyer who will enjoy a superior standard of living very soon after leaving university? Isn't it fair that they pay for what will clearly be a personal benefit? This argument carried significant weight in Australia when fees were re-introduced in 1989 (Independent Committee of Inquiry into Student Finance 1999) and influenced many Labour MPs in the UK in 2004.

It is, however, important to highlight the benefits of higher education that may extend to non-participants. Higher education results in public as well as private benefits (Calhoun 2006; Brennan and Naidoo 2007). Public benefits may include contributions to the local economy, advancing scientific knowledge and engaging in social critique: referred to by Brennan and Naidoo as 'taking truth to power' (2007: 34). In terms of the contribution of higher education to economic regeneration in the UK, it is said to be worth £45 billion annually: a greater contribution than that made by the pharmaceutical industry (*Times Higher* 2008c).

In a sense it can be argued that most graduates (at least those who remain in the UK and who do not die prematurely) will repay their debt to the state through the general taxation system. Those whose degree facilitates entry to lucrative careers will become higher rate taxpayers and may well end up paying more than the real cost of their studies through additional taxation. Other graduates who are less successful, as well as those who make careers in lower paid but essential public services, will pay proportionally less, but they can be seen as repaying their debt through sacrificing personal benefits. Indeed, it could be argued that if the government truly believes that the graduate labour market will provide opportunities for around half of the future labour force, its investment will pay dividends that will benefit all. As an economist, Barr (2001) disagrees, arguing that education is a private as well as a public investment and therefore the individual should bear some of the direct costs. To take an industrial analogy, the owner of a manufacturing firm might argue that the taxpayer should pay for the cost of upgrading his or her machinery as this will increase profitability and, ultimately, be reflected in their tax bill. Barr suggests that some tax relief might be regarded as legitimate, but as the investment does potentially involve private gains it should therefore involve private exposure to risk.

If we accept that the individual should make a contribution to the cost of their education, we are still left with the question of what proportion they should pay (in other words, what are the relative gains to the individual and society?), when they should be expected to pay and, if any payment is to be deferred, how they should pay it back. To take the first question, it is clear that benefits can be linked to the type of course studied and the institution attended. A social science degree from Oxbridge is worth more than a social science degree from most new universities and, irrespective of the institution attended, studying law is likely to yield greater economic returns to the individual than taking a degree in teaching. At the same time, given that the teachers' contribution to the public good may be superior, should we require them to make an equal contribution (as is the case in the UK) or should we recognize these differences through fee variations (as in Australia)?

The issue of payment is particularly significant here as upfront payment may deter the less well-off student from seeking access to high-cost courses that have the potential to yield greatest personal benefits (especially if they lack a familiarity with the potential benefits of particular careers through familial exposure). Indeed, research conducted in Scotland has shown that potential students from working-class families seek out the forms of study that have the lowest overall costs even when immediate costs may be similar for high-value and low-value options (Forsyth and Furlong 2000, 2003).

Perhaps the mistake here, as Barr (2001) suggests, is to focus on the position of applicants and the costs of courses, rather than on the benefits that accrue to graduates. A graduate tax has the potential to provide a level financial playing field for students while the state collects from graduates in proportion to their eventual gain. This removes another potential injustice associated with means-tested grants and fee waivers: the disadvantaged student who becomes a barrister and makes huge personal gains may pay very little for their education while the middle-class student who becomes a teacher and makes far fewer personal gains may have to live with a large educational debt. While Barr (2001) supports the idea of a graduate tax that potentially offers greatest support to those whose degree confers least in the way of personal economic returns, he does recognize the potential for another inequity in which high-earners whose income benefits are not clearly linked to their educational experiences are forced to make high returns under an income contingent system. For Barr, the 'Mick Jagger problem' underlines this inequity. Jagger was registered for a time as a student of accountancy at the LSE, although few would suggest that his subsequent career success was linked to his experience in higher education. Under a system of graduate tax, Jagger would be faced with a large additional tax bill that may be regarded as unfair. While the potential injustice for the extremely wealthy could easily be addressed through a cap on repayments, it could be argued that, ultimately, payment regimes need to be designed to ensure fair access for the masses with a concern for the minority of extremely rich beneficiaries being secondary.

Anticipating debt

These days, in many countries, young people who contemplate becoming students must consider the likely costs of educational participation and reflect on how they can meet any upfront or ongoing costs. They may also want to take account of total costs and potential future earnings to make judgements about the overall value of their course. The cost of study is likely to have the greatest deterrent effect where the potential student feels unable to ask their family to help or where, due to a lack of familiarity with higher education, is either unsure about alternative sources of support or has little information about likely returns and their ability to meet debt out of future earnings (Forsyth and Furlong 2000; Connor et al. 2001; Christie and Munro 2003; Cooke et al. 2004).

In the West of Scotland study, young people were asked about the ways in which the cost of higher education impacted on their decisions about progress. It was clear that many made decisions about progression without having access to accurate information about sources of funding, the levels of contribution expected or about mechanisms for repayment. Indeed, awareness of financial issues was poor and there was a lot of misinformation with some deciding not to progress due to anticipated financial problems. While the majority of respondents subsequently discovered that they were either exempt from fees[12] or eligible for significant discounts, at the stage when they were making educational plans, few had a clear idea of the levels of support that would be available. There were even examples of students who would be fully exempt from fees on account of family income believing that they might be required to pay upfront fees of several thousand pounds before they would be allowed inside the door of a university. With applications for support being made after the offer of a university or college place has been accepted, young people must frequently make spending decisions without being provided with information on costs or sources of support. In this context, Callender (2003) has shown that the complexity of funding arrangements and lack of certainty over arrangements can impede entry, especially for older students, those from low income families and those with dependants.

The complexity of funding policies mean that 'prospective students need to do sophisticated analysis' (Mitton 2007: 378) to calculate likely income or understand the implications of their choices of institution. While students from less well-off families require clear indications of likely levels of support, funds are administered by a range of organizations, each of which operate under different regulations (Mitton 2007). Although there was a great deal of uncertainty about levels of individual support that could be expected among the (largely working-class) Scottish cohort, other evidence suggests that sixth-formers are reasonably accurate in their estimations of accumulated debt, with a slight tendency to over-estimate (NatWest Bank 2006). Indeed, despite the introduction of a number of changes in the funding regime, forecasts tend to be faithful to trends (Figure 3.3). Importantly

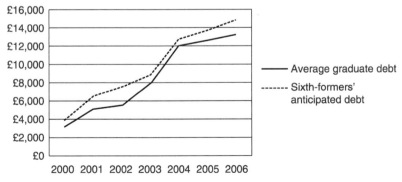

Figure 3.3 Trends in average and anticipated debt, 2000–06, in the UK

Source: NatWest Bank (2006).

though, there is evidence suggesting that young people from the lowest social classes and lone parents are more likely to over-estimate debt and are more debt averse (Callender 2003; Callender and Jackson 2005). According to Callender (2003), the most debt-adverse groups include those from low-income families, lone parents, Muslims and black and minority groups. Compared to debt-adverse groups, those who were debt tolerant were one and a quarter times more likely to enter higher education.

Despite poor knowledge of funding issues, some members of the West of Scotland sample were quite proactive during their final year at school and sought out information on funding from a range of sources. While final details could not be confirmed until much later, they overcame their initial fears and went ahead with their applications despite financial uncertainty:

> [Concern about affordability] made me consider whether or not to go to university, but it was really only for a short time. I thought about it and I found out about what I was going to have to pay and how I was going to organize myself. I found out that I can support myself through the loan. The only thing they didn't do was tell me if I was going to pay fees or not, or if I'll be able to get a good loan, or won't get a good loan. Things like that. I didn't know anything about that until I was actually at university in the course, and then I found out.
>
> (Sheena)

While some were quite resourceful when it came to organizing finances and locating information, there were cases where the opportunity to progress to higher education was rejected due to fear of future debt and concern about the strain that further study would put upon themselves and their families. One young woman, for example, suggested that the issue of affordability was a major deterrent for both herself and her peers:

> North Coaltoun is quite hard hit by unemployment and things like that, so most people think 'Oh! I can't go to university because I have not got the money', and things like that. So maybe if they gave a little bit more financial support to people in that situation they might get more people from areas like North Coaltoun coming to university.
>
> (Maureen)

In Callender's (2003) study of student finance and debt, four out of five respondents believed that the debt that was linked to participation in higher education and had a deterrent effect. Similarly, Connor and colleagues (2001) found that decisions about whether to attend university were affected by financial issues, although for qualified young people who decided against university, affordability tended not to be the prime disincentive. Among less well-off students, the sums involved can be daunting. Newspaper reports that describe students leaving university with debts of well over £10,000 can be extremely frightening to young people who live in households struggling to survive on benefits or poverty-level incomes.[13] As some students pointed out, the sums some owe on graduation would be almost sufficient to buy a small flat in one of the deprived peripheral estates of Glasgow or in one of the ex-mining communities in East Ayrshire. Indeed, sums that might be afford-able to middle-income families can be too large to contemplate in families trying to survive on the poverty line and young people sometimes made decisions to forgo higher education or opted for short courses because they realized what a strain continued education would put on their families. As one young woman put it:

> I mean, you have to look at reality, my mum is a single parent, you know what I mean? Some people just can't afford it, it isn't fair, but that's just the way it is.
>
> (Avril)

In communities where young people still tend to leave school at an early stage, are expected to help provide for their families and still mix with peers who are earning a wage and are able to enjoy a reasonable leisure lifestyle, there is a clear disincentive to participate in post-compulsory education, with higher education seen by some as a step too far. One young woman who decided not to progress to higher education, hated the idea of being reliant on her family for 'pocket money' and felt that she ought to make a contribu-tion to the family finances.

> I hate having to take money off my Mum and Dad. I like being independent and doing my own stuff. Like, I have got a car and that to pay for and if I was not working then I could not afford it.
>
> (Emma)

Parents themselves play an important part in the offspring's decisions about higher education. With few of the parents of the West of Scotland respond-ents having any direct knowledge of higher education, information was poor and young people sometimes had to convince their parents about value of a university education. However, most parents were supportive and more than willing to make sacrifices to help their son or daughter access higher educa-tion in the belief that it was a key to future security and to a higher standard of living. Others were less sure: 'I mean, that's what my Mum and Dad keep saying to me, "Just think of the debt you'll get into" and that' (Lucy).

While the fear of debt and the issue of affordability lead some qualified students to reject the possibility of participating in higher education, others develop strategies which facilitate progression. These strategies, which frequently result in stratified or less intense modes of engagement, are explored in the next section.

Studying within their means

It is difficult to exaggerate the extent to which student experiences are determined by socio-economic circumstances. Those who decide not to pursue higher education, on the grounds of cost, tend to be drawn from working-class families. Moreover, the institutions that students attend and the courses on which they enrol are only partly determined by qualifications. Leaving aside the possible impact of the introduction of differential fees, access to financial resources have a direct effect both on the institutions that young people attend and their choice of courses.

Recognizing that higher education is a costly process and appreciating that parents are unlikely to be able to offer much in the way of financial assistance, students from less-advantaged families need to develop clear strategies to allow them to study within their means. This tends to involve a recognition of the need to combine study with a job, but can sometimes go beyond this with some wanting the additional security of savings or skills to reduce financial risk. In the West of Scotland sample some took time out between school and university to work so as to save money to help them through university, or to get skills that would allow access to jobs paying above the minimum wage.

> Well, partly the reason I took the year out was because of the student loan being introduced. My parents can't afford to support me so I am saving up this year so that I have some money behind me when I do go away.
>
> (Linzi)

The most straightforward strategy to ensure that it was possible to study within their means involved choosing courses at institutions closest to home to limit travel costs so they could remain at home throughout their studies and perhaps retain existing part-time jobs. With housing costs representing the greatest expenditure for students (Royal Bank of Scotland 2007), moving away from home to study is simply not an option for many poorer students. Obviously this limits the choices of the poorest students and represents a powerful form of educational stratification. As we will argue in Chapter 4, home-based students miss out on many of the social and cultural benefits of higher education and, as a result, may be less able to compete with their middle-class peers on the graduate labour market. For those who are able to consider moving, both housing costs and potential part-time earnings display a large regional variation: rent in Aberdeen or London, for example, is almost twice as expensive as Sheffield, while average hourly earnings in London (£8.67) are significantly higher than in Leicester (£5.08) (Royal Bank of Scotland 2007).

Considerations of cost not only deter less advantaged students from accessing opportunities in the national educational market place, but can even serve to restrict local choices. Some West of Scotland students even chose a place of study on the basis of relatively small daily savings in travel costs: there were examples of young people who chose a less prestigious institution within a city simply because it saved them an extra daily bus fare rather than because they preferred the institution or the courses on offer.

Daily commuting from the parental home both helped minimize the accommodation costs that can form a major part of the expense of higher education as well as providing continued access to parental support. Young people often entered into agreements with their family, which recognized both their own hardships and their parents' inability to provide for their needs as students:

> I don't pay money and they don't give me money, we kind of agreed on that you know, that's fine.
>
> (Audrey)

> If I am working, I will pay money to my Mum and Dad, aye, but if I am not then they just give me free rent.
>
> (Sheena)

In this way, parents were able to provide support for their sons and daughters without having to part with cash, while students used loans and money from part-time jobs to pay for all directly incurred costs such as books, travel, clothes and leisure.

Another strategy used by less advantaged students to enable them to study within their means involved enrolling on short courses, especially those that conferred eligibility for bursaries, such as HNCs, or had preferential funding arrangements, such as nursing. Several respondents expressed a preference for courses with a strong vocational emphasis. As we suggest in Chapter 4, for less-advantaged students, higher education tends to be seen as an investment with expenditure justified in terms of clear and calculable career advantage.

In these circumstances, young people from less-advantaged families often seek out courses with clear career linkages. They can be reluctant to take courses like English or History as, aside from school teaching, they cannot easily see what they would use them for. The risks are too great. These tendencies help explain the attraction of health-related subjects as these subjects have clear career linkages, are sometimes shorter courses and often have superior funding arrangements. From medicine and dentistry to nursing and physiotherapy there were obvious career linkages: young people knew what they were going to be doing at the end, which was important to them. With some of the health professions having moved towards degree level entry relatively recently, students who were first generation higher education entrants often knew someone in the health professions whereas aside from their teachers, they often had little first-hand knowledge of other graduate careers.

Student reflections on funding arrangements

With students directly faced with the consequences of funding policies, not surprisingly they and their representatives have strong views about the equity of regimes and the desirability of reforms. In England, the decision to increase fees in 2004 led to widespread protests, while in Scotland, where fees were abolished very soon after being introduced, following promises made by the Scottish Nationalist government, the re-introduction of student grants is now back on the political agenda.[14]

Students frequently complain about the difficulties in making ends meet and about the need to work long hours in order to get by and, understandably, they frequently regard funding policies as having a detrimental effect on their standard of living. In the West of Scotland study, course fees caused a great deal of resentment, but fees had been introduced relatively recently and the requirement for some to pay up front clearly caused hardship. Students also compare their own situations with those encountered by recent participants (perhaps with brothers and sisters) who enjoyed a more favourable funding regime. With primary and secondary education being free for all, there was a widespread feeling that the state should either cover the full costs of study or should ensure that higher education was available at the point of use without any upfront charges.

The West of Scotland students were also aware of issues of social justice, particularly the extent to which those from poorer families were adversely affected by current funding policies. A sense of injustice was provoked by the realization that, for some, educational choices were adversely affected by family circumstances while, for others, family resources opened doors and provided the means through which young people could live a student-centred life to the full. Among the affluent students included in Christie and Munro's (2003) study, several had the entire costs of their study covered by their parents, with some of these better-off students taking their financial advantages for granted and giving little thought to the equity of funding policies. In contrast, several young people in the West of Scotland study had a clear sense of injustice and believed that some were excluded from university due to their families' financial situation: 'There's a lot of folk that could go to uni but cannae go because they've no money to go' (Laurie).

Aware of broader debates about affordability in a national context and familiar with the contrasts between the financial situations of different groups of students, several students in the West of Scotland study supported a policy of means testing. Others made the distinction between fees (which were widely regarded as unjust) and grants which some thought should be related to family income:

> Well, I wouldn't give everyone grants because, I mean, there are people that don't need it.
>
> (Angus)

> Well, if I was part of the government I would bring back grants . . . I would make sure that everyone was treated equally, no matter how much [money] their parents made.
>
> (William)

A sense of injustice was also related to the more advantageous funding regimes applicable to certain (often lower-level) courses. Student nurses, for example, are paid a training wage and therefore removed from the loans regime. Students on sub-degree courses in further education colleges are frequently eligible for bursaries; seen by some as rewarding those who 'bummed about' in secondary school.

Conclusion

Policies relating to the financial support of students have a direct bearing on processes of stratification and hence relate directly to issues of social justice. In countries with mass systems of higher education, the impact of financial support packages on stratification can be somewhat obscure because their impact on overall entry patterns is relatively low compared to their impact on the distribution of students between institutions and courses. In other words, funding in itself may not be a major deterrent, but is linked to stratification of the student experience and, ultimately, to broader processes of social reproduction. Indeed, while different countries adopt a variety of approaches to funding higher education, from market-based to social approaches, in their own ways, they all protect social advantage.

Given strong differences in the ability and willingness of families to support their offspring through higher education, any approach that requires family contributions to either fees or living costs would seem incompatible with social justice. Under the current funding regimes in the UK, those from affluent families have more choices and ultimately enjoy a very different student experience. While wealthy families are likely to ensure that their offspring enjoy a good standard of living whatever system is in place, it is important that the poorest students can live independently throughout their studies without contributions from parents and without excessive labour market engagement.

If family contributions are ruled out on the grounds of social justice and if individual beneficiaries are to shoulder a proportion of the costs, then repayment mechanisms need to be designed so that they neither deter entry nor encourage less well-off students to seek out low-cost products. With debt aversion varying between socio-economic and ethnic groups, some form of pooling of costs and a repayment system based on benefit is perhaps the fairest system. Here a graduate tax levy payable by all graduates based on income would ensure that all beneficiaries contribute in accordance with their net gains.

4

Fragmented contexts

[Y]oung people entering 'mass' higher education are certainly not
blind to class-based inequalities and discriminatory behaviour. Policy
needs to address more directly the muddle and disincentives in the
financing of educational studies, and the stress of juggling competing
demands in the short duration UK full-time degree. It also needs to
recognize more generously that it takes considerable self belief and
courage for people from disadvantaged social backgrounds to make
their way even in the most open of UK higher education institutions
under present labour market and policy conditions.

(Evans 2002: 52)

Introduction

While students in higher education engage in learning at an advanced level
in specific disciplines or follow courses leading to higher-level vocational or
professional competencies, the application of the label 'student' to an individual suggests a certain uniformity of status and experience that no longer
reflects underlying reality. The student body is divided in a range of ways,
perhaps more strongly linked to underlying differences in the reputation or
scarcity of the educational 'product' and predicted future outcomes than to
course specific requirements or modes of delivery associated with different
disciplines.

There are a multitude of divisions that result in the stratification of the
student experience, including the division between 'old' and 'new' universities and the further education sector, between prestigious and less prestigious courses, between students living at home and those who have moved
to study and between those who enjoy student-focused lifestyles and those
who must combine study with extensive engagement in employment-related
activities. These divisions are significant in a number of ways: employers may
favour degrees from certain institutions, some specialisms open the doors to

particularly rewarding careers while others tend to provide routes into lower-paid sectors of the economy. Moreover, contexts can be significant, providing access to informal networks, an introduction to middle-class lifestyles and assumptive worlds and providing different opportunities for the enhancement of social capital (Brennan and Osborne 2008). Importantly, the various forms of stratification that fragment the student experience relate directly to labour market experiences and the reproduction of class-based inequalities. A studentship is effectively a tiered experience that builds and maintains class divisions among the new workforce. As Ozga and Sukhnanadan observe, 'one-dimensional' images of 'the student' are no longer meaningful (1998: 319).

In this chapter we examine some of the key forms of stratification in the student experience and look at the distinctive forms of engagement linked to various divisions. We argue that, in different ways, the fragmentation of experience effectively ensures that those from less well-off families have distinct, and in many ways poorer, higher educational experiences, even when they manage to secure access to prestigious courses in elite institutions. Indeed, we can identify a range of mechanisms that help ensure that wider access does not result in a more open class structure or pose a threat to the reproduction of class advantage.

Old versus new

Some of the most salient divisions in the student experience can be linked to the education policies that were introduced in the 1960s to encourage and manage wider access. As we saw earlier, whereas the Robbins Report had envisaged expansion of the university sector to meet increased demand for higher education and provide a workforce suited to the needs of the new economy, the Secretary of State, Tony Crosland, who was deeply suspicious of the universities, proposed a binary system in which 30 polytechnics were introduced to provide a different (but not inferior) form of higher education closely linked to the perceived needs of industry and technology. Ironically, Crosland's aim was to increase opportunities and break down class divisions, although he effectively created the conditions that helped ensure that the growth in working-class participation was contained within a separate set of structures that ultimately helped protect middle-class advantage. Crosland, who announced the changes by remarking 'Let us now move away from our snobbish caste-ridden hierarchical obsession with university status' (Crosland 1982: 159), would have been deeply disappointed.

Although the polytechnics achieved university status in 1992, clear distinctions remain. The ex-polytechnics, commonly referred to as the 'new' universities, have maintained a greater range of vocational and vocationally relevant courses and tend to run a combination of degree level and advanced sub-degree courses. Until a recent trade union merger, staff in the new universities were members of different unions and were on different pay scales.

Teaching contact hours tended to be higher in the new universities, research activity lower and (partly due to the link between research and overall income) per capita funding inferior. As we showed in Chapter 2, the socio-economic profile of students in the new university sector differs strongly from the established sector: students are drawn from lower-income families, tend to have significantly poorer entrance qualifications and tend to reside locally. High prestige courses, such as medicine and dentistry, tend not to be offered at new universities and course portfolios are still skewed towards vocational subjects.

With the binary divide helping to maintain a class-based distinction in higher education throughout a period of expansion, up until the recession of the early 1980s (which led to a significant increase in unemployment, especially among young people), a traditional university education still represented the final rung of a ladder of selection that virtually guaranteed access to professional and managerial positions and to middle-class lifestyles. Yet while students in the traditional universities were drawn predominantly from middle-class families, those working-class students who gained access to the established universities did tend to be full participants who emerged from their studies subjectively prepared for middle-class life (Ashton and Field 1976). It is true that many initially experienced the university as an alien cultural environment (e.g. Jackson and Marsden 1966; Ostrove 2003), but university life often involved a total immersion and it was difficult to remain uninvolved. The student peer group often formed the basis for patterns of sociability and, with many students studying away from home, residential proximity and the lack of an established network within a city helped forge new friendships that crossed class boundaries.

Student life tended to revolve around the university and participants encountered the same small peer group on a daily basis in lectures and tutorials. In their studies, students had regular small group (or even individual) tutorials with a member of staff who tracked their progress and assessed their work. In a sense, the system represented a middle-class apprenticeship in which the student had the ongoing support of an experienced practitioner (the tutor) as well as the company of a group of peers who were in the process of developing similar skills. Moreover, within a relatively stable occupational world, with the help of tutors and peers, students were able to build a fairly accurate picture of the nature of the graduate labour market and their own position within it.

From the mid-1980s, the pace of growth began to increase which required a range of institutional adaptations. Even within the traditional university sector, expansion resulted in the incorporation of new groups. The number of mature students increased as women returning to the labour market sought new opportunities while workers made redundant due to the recession and process of industrial transformation saw university degrees as providing a foundation for new careers. Many of these new students were the first in their families to enter university.

Against this backdrop, expectations and experiences began to change.

Mass participation meant that higher education was incorporated into the frames of reference of young people from a variety of backgrounds and came to represent a finishing school for middle-class and aspiring youth. For many, the experience of being a student, a status linked to youthful lifestyles and freedom from the ties of full-time employment, was more of a draw than the attraction of advanced study or immersion in a discipline to further knowledge. Whereas students in the established universities once regarded themselves as budding intellectuals, as future professionals or senior managers, today, even in the ancient universities, young people may drift through university only marginally interested in their subjects and without giving much thought to life after university.

With rising numbers, a university education ceased to resemble a middle-class apprenticeship. Teaching became anonymized and personal links with full-time tutors replaced with fleeting contact with casual staff and postgraduate teaching assistants (especially in the first year). In the established universities, students are far more likely to be taught by casual staff (Sastry and Bekhradnia 2007). Referred to by Scanlon and colleagues (2007) as a 'lean and mean pedagogy', it is argued large lecture groups and the lack of close contact with staff mean that intimate bonds between students and their institutions never develop (Smith and Webster 1997; Scanlon et al. 2007). In modern university settings, lecturing staff may have little knowledge of the personal circumstances of their students and may not even know their names (a situation that might partly be associated with the introduction of anonymous marking), while new students may experience a 'lack of connectedness' (Perry and Allard 2003). Scanlon and colleagues also suggest alienation from the institution can be reinforced by their lack of close involvement with other students. In the new higher educational environment, the world of the student has become semi-detached from the world of the academy. Moreover, new divisions have opened up within the student body relating not simply to academic disciplines but to patterns of residence, to levels of disposable income and to types of engagement with the world of work.

While all universities have been forced to change, the new universities continue to offer a very different set of experiences to those provided by the established universities (Teichler 2004; Brennan and Osborne 2008). In many senses they are more supportive of working-class students: they offer courses that are more familiar and which make sense in occupational terms and they may provide greater assistance to students who lack study skills. To an extent, they have to be more supportive as many of their students are unprepared academically for advanced study (in terms of UCAS points of entrants, the average entry tariff at Cambridge University is 517 compared to 187 at the new university of East London (*Sunday Times* 2008)).[1]

Over time, the new universities have come to appreciate the distinctive nature of their market and have begun to sell themselves in ways that fit with the aspirations of working-class students. They stress the relevance of their curriculum, their links with industry and the employability of their graduates. Unlike the established universities which may promote their reputation as part of their sales technique, the new universities engage in a hard sell and make extensive use of advertisements that speak directly to their demographic. Using a working-class 'voice-over', Napier University in Edinburgh, for example, recently ran a series of television adverts in which it clearly presents itself as an institution offering a preparation for practical semi-professional occupations rather than preparation for higher professional or academic careers. This message is reinforced on its website where it states:

> The majority of our courses are vocational – that means they focus on the practical – teaching you skills that employers look for. It's not just about getting you a degree.
>
> (www.napier.ac.uk, accessed 17 July 2007)

In turn, the established universities use more subtle marketing techniques that centre around age, tradition and exclusivity. They frequently showcase the achievements of their alumni (which may include prime ministers and famous scientists) and emphasize their self-proclaimed scientific and cultural superiority. While new universities must put great effort into recruiting students, the established universities are in a position where they can select from an over-supply of qualified applicants (MacLennan et al. 2000). Illustrating the emphasis universities place on image and branding, Fearn argues that 'a Russell Group university should not market itself like a post-1992 university. It's got a very different sort of message and needs to dress in a very different way' (2008: 42). Indeed, she describes how Southampton University (an established university) recently changed its logo (which featured a dolphin) out of a concern that it might be mistaken for a post-1992 university.

The significance of these marketing techniques should not be overlooked as they play a crucial role in the reproduction of advantage through shaping class-based choices. Highlighting the link between young people's class-based identities and institutional preferences, Ball and colleagues suggest that decisions about which institutions to apply for are linked to lifestyle choices which 'are infused with class and ethnic meaning' (2002: 51). As a result of a series of highly publicized national surveys relating to different aspects of the student experience (from satisfaction with assessment and feedback to the cost of a pint of beer), universities themselves are aware of the complex balance between academic and social factors that influence student choices: a recent survey for the *Times Higher Educational Supplement* (2007b) suggests that social aspects are particularly important. From a sociological perspective, Croxford and Raffe (2005) have highlighted the significance of market structures for processes of social closure, while Ball and colleagues (2000, 2002) provide rich illustration of the ways in which the choices that are embedded in self-reflexive biographies (Beck 1992) help reproduce inequalities.

Despite professing a commitment to the principles of social justice, the marketing strategies employed by different universities clearly exploit their knowledge of class-based differences in taste in order to boost recruitment from their preferred demographic. While the older universities stress conservatism and high culture, the new universities frequently seek to portray a 'down-to-earth' and accessible image. In this context, Ball and colleagues (2002) describe the ways in which the middle classes were suspicious of universities who advertised (seen as 'desperate') and show how certain advertising strategies can backfire among particular groups of students (some of their respondents, for example, were put off by institutions that emphasized the social aspects of student life over the academic). Similarly in a study of students' perceptions of different aspects of a university's 'brand', Bennett and Ali-Choudhury (forthcoming) argued that the class and ethnic composition of the student body affected impressions about the institution. Those from 'non-traditional' backgrounds appeared to be most at ease with institutions where such students were well represented.

The marketing messages promoted by the different universities provide clear signals about the social class positions and aspirations of existing and potential students. If student choices are linked to perceptions about class-based authenticity (Reay 2007), then branding exercises are about maintaining a class-based consumer profile. Of course, the new universities have developed out of a very different tradition and their educational 'products' are distinct (Brennan and Osborne 2008). Courses at sub-degree level have co-existed with degree courses and channels between qualification levels have often been kept open. Many of the courses now offered at degree level in the new universities were once sub-degree courses and have only recently been linked to bachelors' qualifications. Programmes frequently have strong industry links and student placements are far more common than in the traditional university sector. The sector has a tradition of teaching working-class students and of attracting and supporting non-traditional applicants. These strengths are often recognized by school teachers who, understandably, may encourage those from less advantaged backgrounds to apply to an institution perceived as having a culture that respects and values working-class traditions and perspectives and which provide ongoing support to less confident students (Forsyth and Furlong 2000).

Institutional hierarchies and the division between the new and old universities are often thought of as representing differences in attainment and academic potential. Yet there is an ongoing debate about the extent to which the ancient universities operate admissions policies that are biased towards those who have been privately educated. The universities argue that they simply recruit the best qualified students, many of whom happen to have been privately educated. Some politicians and public commentators argue that admissions interviews favour those with the confidence that can be linked to a middle-class upbringing and to the social capital that helps smooth processes of social reproduction. There is a lack of hard evidence to support the idea of overt interviewer bias, although in a survey of 10,000 privately educated applicants suggested that privileged applicants frequently found Oxbridge admissions interviews rude and aggressive (*The Telegraph* 2001); it would be surprising if working-class applicants did not regard interviews with middle-class Dons as intimidating.

The reality of admissions to elite institutions is complex and goes beyond judgements about qualifications or assessments about the potential ability of an applicant to overcome disadvantage. Affordability is an important issue for those who are unable to contemplate moving away to study, but also because working-class (and even lower middle-class) students can feel uneasy in educational environments dominated by affluent students and may make choices that reflect their class positions (Ball et al. 2002; Reay 2007). Commenting on the fairness of admissions processes, the Principal of St Hugh's College at Oxford University, Andrew Dilnot, admitted that there was a problem persuading some qualified young people to apply due to a misapprehension that they would be entering an unfamiliar social environment. In Dilnot's words, 'they fear they will be surrounded by people who are socially different, and I feel powerfully that they're wrong about that' (*The Guardian* 2007). Dilnot perhaps needs to get out more and visit other universities to appreciate just how wrong he is. Indeed, some of his own students would disagree with his views. One recent Oxford graduate wrote an article in *The Guardian* suggesting that there was a need to recruit more 'normal' students and arguing that Oxford 'is meant to be a university not a finishing school half stocked with uneasy plebs wondering what the hell went wrong' (quoted in the *Times Higher* 2008a). Clearly these issues do not simply reflect bias on the part of the older universities, consumer choice plays a key role and is driven not just by judgements of long-term benefits but by impressions of differences in the student experience and by perceptions of the 'fit' between class-based identities and institutional images (Ball et al. 2002; Reay 2007).

In the West of Scotland study, young people frequently said that the reputation of institutions was linked to the decision to apply, although typically reputation and location were mentioned in the same sentence. For some, an institution's reputation was signalled by its age. One young man suggested that Glasgow University was well run, was well established and had a 'big history'. Another, commenting on new universities, said, 'It's not that they're not good, . . . but . . . because they've been built recently, they kind of need to build up their reputation'. Although reputation clearly had some impact on application decisions, for less advantaged applicants, choices were typically limited to those institutions that were close enough to make daily commuting possible. Indeed, a recent survey by MORI (2005) showed that the majority of young people from professional and managerial families regarded institutional reputation as the most important factor influencing choice of institution, whereas those from other social classes placed far less emphasis on reputation.

The physical environment and architecture could also be important, but there were different views about various attributes. For some, universities were supposed to look old and imposing: grand buildings in themselves underlined the reputation. However, those from less-advantaged families frequently spoke of the intimidating feel of the established universities, described by one as having a 'stern appearance', and often associated 'grand' built environments with the upper middle classes. In contrast, modern concrete environments were often seen as much more familiar and even inviting.

Reputations are established in a variety of ways and are sometimes linked to the perceived approachability of staff and friendliness of fellow students. Here respondents often made explicit contrasts between the old and new universities with such impressions being reinforced through open days and through word of mouth. Some of the young people in the West of Scotland study experienced both types of institution, moving from old to new due to dissatisfaction with the former.

Staff in the new universities were generally regarded as being more friendly and approachable and willing to spend time helping students with a variety of problems. In contrast, several described the staff in older institutions as culturally remote, as one young woman described an ancient Scottish university, 'It is an old uni and it's got old, if you know what I'm trying to say. It was a wee bit too snobbish for me in some ways.' One young man who transferred from an old to a new university talked about being too scared to talk to staff in the established university about his problems in case he got 'booted out': at the new university he felt that there was 'a lot less pressure' arguing that 'it's a lot easier to get on and there's a lot more help'. Among some who experienced established universities there was a feeling of being an imposter in an alien world and a subliminal concern about being 'found out', while others highlighted difficulties communicating with staff.

> I think that when you do approach them [staff at an established university], they are so intelligent in a way that they don't know how to respond to your questions in simple terms. So there is no point in going to see them because it doesn't help you.
>
> (Brian)

At new universities, students tended to feel more of a cultural affinity with staff and felt much more relaxed about talking to them. As one young man put it, 'If you are having troubles, you can go and see the head of department and talk away to them.' Another young man at an established university who had friends studying at a new university commented on the benefits of smaller scale and greater contact:

> I've got quite a lot of friends at xxx [new university] and they say that the whole class is smaller so it's more personalized. You sort of know your lecturer more, he'll probably know your name and I think that would make it easier to go and see him. And from what I've heard, the lecturers are younger and more helpful.
>
> (Rab)

The cultural gulf that could impact on relationships between working-class students and lecturers also affected patterns of peer interaction. From the perspective of working-class students, differences in accent were crucial markers of social status that marked out potential friendship networks. Even basic conversation could be difficult and marked by misunderstandings. Perceptions of socio-economic differences affected institutional choices. Young people spoke about being able to relate to fellow students at the new universities and of being afraid to open their mouths at the ancient universities. As one young woman put it:

> You want to be able to enjoy your time at uni and want to be able to talk to people without feeling that you don't want to open your mouth in class because of your accent.

> (Evelyn)

Another young woman was quite clear that she applied to a new university because she thought that the 'common background' would result in 'a better social life' while some of those who had entered new universities commented directly on the class background of their classmates:

> I don't think that if you come from the East End that you fit in at *** [traditional] university. I think that if you could do a course at *** [new] university or somewhere, you are probably better doing that than coming here . . . It's just everybody's, it's just they've got a different background than you.

> (Ellen)

While cultural differences clearly represent a significant barrier, there is also an awareness of different approaches to learning. Partly linked to differences in the subject ranges offered but also embedded in established pedagogies, the older universities tend to adopt an approach that involves a low level of staff–student contact with independent learning playing a more central role (Blackmore 1997; Barnett 2003; Sastry and Bekhradnia 2007). This devolved approach to learning results not just in weak links between staff and students, but also inhibits interaction between students, especially in the early years when mass lecture-based teaching predominates. Several students in the West of Scotland group mentioned the small number of other students that they knew and the fleeting contact they had with others. One spoke of being 'thrown in the deep end . . . going to a lecture then going home and doing the rest yourself'. Another mentioned that her few student friends 'were never in at the same time as me so I found myself just wandering about and going to the library, and I didn't like that'. Although driven by resources, the shift towards less intensive staff–student interactions is often justified in terms of modern pedagogies which place an emphasis on self-directed learning (Kirkup 1996; Barnett 2003): disparagingly referred to by the National Union of Students as a FOFO ('Fuck off and find out') approach (Allen and Ainley 2007).

What comes across very clearly is that factors that lead to institutional stratification go far beyond entrance qualifications and involve a set of influences that, in a range of ways, pertain to social class and reinforce socio-economic divisions. The students themselves are actively involved in the choices that help reproduce advantage and disadvantage (Reay et al. 2005).

While politicians highlight biased admissions procedures, most selection takes places at an earlier stage and are influenced not only by class cultures but are shaped by the marketing strategies used by institutions to reach out to their preferred demographic as well as by students' own assessments of the quality of the social life associated with different institutions (*Times Higher Education Supplement* 2007b).

Disciplinary status and consumer demand

The academic–vocational divide represents an important division in higher education and helps mark a differentiation between the worlds of advantaged and less-advantaged students. With a greater emphasis on vocational courses within the new universities (some of which are offered at sub-degree level), subject choices reinforce the institutional separation of working-class and middle-class students. However, within the established universities there are also divisions that relate to the prestige of courses; differences that also reinforce social stratification. Again these divisions are not solely about entry qualifications but reflect the confidence of applicants, their willingness to immerse themselves in an unfamiliar cultural world, their ability to convince admissions tutors that their 'face fits' and their access to funds that facilitate an extended educational engagement.

Among less-advantaged students who take up places in the established universities, there tends to be an awareness that some courses have a particular appeal to those from very affluent families and attract a strong over-representation of privately educated students. These courses include the obvious ones linked to highly paid professions such as medicine, dentistry, veterinary science and law as well as those without any obvious career linkages such as history of art or classics. In one study, Skeggs (1997) noted that working-class girls placed a priority on practical skills (often involving care) while rejecting more academic subjects as 'useless'. This was a process that was also clearly evident among the West of Scotland sample. Having little confidence in their academic abilities, it was not uncommon for young people to downgrade their aspirations, to aim for something they saw as a little less demanding (perhaps at sub-degree level) or accept a college place rather than making direct transitions from school to university (perhaps with the hope of upgrading from sub-degree to degree courses at a later stage).

For qualified applicants the dilemma is that some of the courses that are in high demand by students from affluent families are ones that are attractive to the less well-off due to their strong career links. On the other hand, it was clear from discussions with members of the West of Scotland study that 'posh' courses, with or without clear career links, were unattractive partly due to the need to mix with students from more advantaged and culturally remote backgrounds:

Philosophy is something that I've always been interested in, but I've never told anybody, you know, because they get this sort of idea, you know where they go, 'huh!', . . . I'm a kid from the East End and when I say that I want to do law, people think 'Christ, you must be from Bearsden' [a 'posh' suburb] or something like that.

(Callum)

Indeed, less-advantaged students were often reluctant to choose courses that lacked clear links to the occupational world, even when they had a strong interest in a non-vocational subject. One young woman, for example, rejected the option of studying subjects she enjoyed and was good at (music and drama) in favour of a vocational course due to concerns about the link to a secure future career:

I would have loved to [have studied music and drama] as soon as I wasn't in school, but it is all to do with confidence. And I thought to myself, what if I am not good enough, what if I don't make it, you know? And then I think, OK, well, let's think about this. So I thought if I go do my medical secretary or whatever I was going to do, I thought at least it is something practical behind me, so that if I did go to drama, then I'm not as good as I think I am, then I have got something to fall back on. I can at least go and, you know, apply for a job to be a medical secretary and say, like, I have got the qualifications for this, could you please give me a job?

(Avril)

Expressing a sentiment shared by several working-class students, one spoke of the risk involved in doing 'degrees for positions that don't exist'. Some also spoke of wanting to do a degree that was 'almost like an apprenticeship' because it removed worry and made the investment safer.

I definitely wanted to do a degree where I knew it would be almost like an apprenticeship because it removed any worry. I was worried I would do an English degree, or something I was interested in [I might not] get a job at the end of it.

(Morag)

Despite a tendency to choose subjects tightly linked to careers and an aversion to courses dominated by upper middle-class students, some members of the West of Scotland study did enrol on courses in which state-educated students were poorly represented, but the need to maintain a distance from 'posh' students was evident among those who had entered high prestige courses at established universities. They were anxious to mark themselves out as being different from their middle-class peers at university and, especially, outside the university. A medical student from a deprived area recounted how she distanced herself from her fellow students and often told strangers that she was a student in another (less prestigious) discipline.

I tend to lie quite a lot. Like, if I am out on a night and people ask you 'What you do?', I'll just say that I am a student, and my friends, a lot of them are engineers, so if I'm out with them I'll just kind of, like, nod when they are saying that they are engineers. I've got more in common with them. I think if I don't say that I'm a medical student, then they'll get a better idea of what kind of person I am.

(Ellen)

While some of the respondents did manage to form close friendships at university, they often remained suspicious of their middle-class peers and regarded them almost as alien beings. Many maintained a keen awareness of social class differences throughout their time at university:

There's definitely a lot more middle-class people and I find that quite strange. There's a lot of, I don't know, we call them 'yahs'. There's a lot of them, they are quite yucky . . . It sounds bad, their accents and they're loud and they just think they're wonderful.

(Elspeth)

At the level of subject choice, again processes of consumer demand clearly remain very influential factors in the maintenance of class-based divisions. Importantly, at this level, some of the most able working-class students, who have overcome a range of obstacles to get to university are avoiding precisely the courses that offer them the greatest chances of long-range social mobility. In many ways, the acceptance of an upper middle-class monopoly in certain courses is at odds with the social justice agenda, yet severe social class imbalances at a course level attract little attention at the political or institutional level.

Home and away

Patterns of social integration within an institution are also strongly affected by residential segregation and reinforced by the tendency of working-class students to continue to live with their parents, often commuting relatively long distances, and to prefer the company of friends in their local communities. Research (MORI 2005) has highlighted this tendency, showing that when it comes to choice of institution, the ability to live at home is twice as important for working-class than for middle-class students, even though three in five feel that students who live at home do not get the full benefit of the student experience. The tendency to remain at home is primarily an economic decision with many students clear that moving away was never seen as an affordable option:

It's too far away [English or Edinburgh institutions], you would have to, like, spend a lot of money, plus you're not guaranteed you are going to get something out of the course for it.

(Chin-Ho)

Yet while there were clearly issues of affordability, some preferred to stay close to family and friends for social and cultural reasons. Lack of confidence about their ability to cope with independent living and being away from family and friends was often compounded by low academic aspirations, feelings of financial insecurity, uncertainties about student life, poor future expectations and a more general underlying lack of confidence. Going to university was a big enough step, without adding other risks:

> I was 18 or whatever and I didnae really want to leave, but I thought xxx ['new' university] is just one bus run out the road and all . . . Really, I didnae just want to leave my parents. I didnae know if I would be able to kind of cope, you know what I mean, I wanted to stay under my own [i.e. parental] roof.
>
> (Ben)

In a recent report by Education Research Services (2007), evidence was presented showing that home-based students had a poor educational experience overall, being less likely to participate in optional parts of their course, such as work placements, reporting feelings of isolation from their fellow students due to limited opportunities for socialization and even being less likely to secure graduate employment. Restricted patterns of socialization among home-based students was also noted in the West of Scotland study and here, at an extreme, an inability or unwillingness to leave home, could even cost a place at university. One young woman, for example, had her only offer from an institution that required her to move away from home, but felt she was not ready to move:

> It would have meant having to move . . . I'm a wimp, I found it a bit scary. I really hadn't got a clue about anything about it. I wouldn't know where to start about getting accommodation or anything like that.
>
> (Kathleen)

While 18 year olds can feel unprepared to move and mature students may be unable to relocate, those who live in remote areas have to leave home if they want to participate in higher education. This can have a strong bearing on decisions about progression, although many young people from rural areas are aware that higher education probably represents their best opportunity to move to the city and participate in what is frequently perceived as an exciting and cosmopolitan urban culture (Cartmel and Furlong 2000).

Student-centred and employment-centred lifestyles

Another powerful mechanism through which the experiences of middle-class and working-class students are stratified relates to patterns of engagement in paid work. While changes in student support have increased the pressure on students from all social classes to combine study with employment, the pressure on students from less-affluent families is particularly acute. With the lives of some students being more employment-focused than study-focused, cross-class socialization becomes even more difficult and being a student comes to mean different things for different socio-economic groups (Callender and Wilkinson 2003; Little 2006). Research by MORI (2005) shows that, on average, employed students work 14.5 hours a week with 14 per cent working more than 20 hours. However, averages conceal some large variations and there is clear evidence showing that working-class students are more likely to be employed during term-time and likely to work longer hours.

The MORI survey showed that while around a third of middle-class students worked during term-time, more than one in two working-class students held jobs. Work engagement among students has increased significantly in recent years, partly as a result of changes in funding arrangements, but also due to an overall increase in students from less well-off families whose parents are unable to subsidize their studies. There is also evidence of an increased demand for student labour by employers who recognize the benefits of recruiting from a pool of flexible labour with strong social skills who are willing to accept minimum wages (Sparrow and Cooper 2003; Wooden and Warren 2003). The trend towards increased student participation in the labour market has also been noted in other countries, such as Australia where, between 1994 and 1999, levels of engagement almost doubled (McInnis et al. 2000).

In the West of Scotland study, some students were working incredibly long hours – sometimes effectively combining full-time study with full-time employment together with long hours commuting:

> I'm working between 40 and 45 hours a week at the moment and my college course is, works out about 18 hours, so I'm going home and I'm sleeping, if not I'm studying, you know it's quite heavy going . . . I've never been so tired. But even if I'm tired I'll come in [to college] and I've never fallen asleep in class.
>
> (Libby)

> Last year I was working . . . quite a lot of hours, ended up in hospital for a week due to stress. So I had to give up that job and now I'm working like half the hours that I was working before and I'm just constantly trying to get money from places . . . I get a loan, ahah!, and I get a scholarship as well, and at the moment I'm trying to get my [absent] dad to pay me money, hah.
>
> (Annie)

Trying to combine study with long hours in employment could lead to fatigue and could impact on academic performance. But employers often put pressure on students to work longer hours, to cover shifts when other workers are absent or to increase working at times of peak demand. The demand from employers at Christmastime, together with the setting of Christmas exams in some institutions could be particularly problematic.

Indeed, many of the larger retail outlets explicitly prohibit staff from taking holidays in December and early January (some even insist that existing employees take on extra hours to cope with the Christmas peak), while universities, perhaps oblivious to the demands placed on employed students, often set exams in January based on the assumption that the Christmas 'break' offers opportunities for revision:

> At Christmastime, when I was working, they [supermarket] were asking me to do overtime and you need the money obviously because it's Christmas. But then you've got exams to study in January. So I'm sort of blaming that on why I failed two of my exams in January.
>
> (Linzie)

Some learned to work around these problems by getting signed off as 'sick' when they needed to put more time into their studies. Others struggled to reconcile study and work and made a decision to abandon their job or their course or to try and find a new balance between them. Despite needing the money, some reluctantly gave up their jobs rather than lose out on class time, despite being aware of the hardships that this could incur:

> It's hard, it's really hard, it's, like, you find a part-time job, and then uni kicks in, and it's, like, you've loads of work to do, so you end up missing hours, end up just saying to the job, nah, I can't stay any more, I've got too much uni stuff to do . . . Oh, you have to, but sometimes you just have to, I mean, when you get a job and you're trying to keep a job, that you put the hours in as well, but it's just a loada hassle, I mean, it costs money travelling between here [campus], the job and your house . . . Yeah, definitely, you need to give up work to go to uni.
>
> (Fergus)

Lecturers added to the pressure by regarding missed lectures or deadlines as a sign of poor commitment and imposing penalties as a way of trying to secure greater involvement and conformity. Little (2006) describes how lecturers reported an increased demand for multiple copies of lecture notes by students who had promised copies for absent peers, and how some lecturers would remove or limit web-based information as a way of trying to enforce traditional modes of engagement. In some respects, it is those who enrol in the most prestigious courses who were most adversely affected. On such courses, especially those with practical or lab-based modules, it is more difficult to avoid regular attendance. High status courses are often longer and involve more direct expenses on items such as books and equipment and terms can be longer; in medicine, for example, there is a summer term that curtails employment opportunities.

> Money is by far the biggest problem. In first year I worked and that was quite hard going . . . When I got into second year, the course goes up quite a few notches so I had to give it up. So I was just living at home and my parents don't give me any money at all, so that's the hardest thing.

And then because I'd saved up some money, second year wasn't so bad, but this year I had already maxed-out my overdraft at the beginning of the year, so I don't know what I'm going to do in the summer. I can't get a summer job because I've got a term this summer, but you can get bank loans out now apparently.

(Ellen)

While students are often thought of as dependent or semi-dependent, some of those in the West of Scotland study had to help provide for their families, especially when they had an unemployed parent. Some students had children to provide for and faced a very different set of experiences:

Right now, I'm having to work two jobs because my girlfriend's just had a wee baby. She's also, she's got another wee boy as well and I'm kind of like his Dad, so the way I see is like trying to support the two of them as well, so I've had to take on this other job as well as doing uni.

(Shug)

Studies of the experiences of mature students highlight such tensions (Edwards 1993; Wisker 1996; Marks et al. 2003; Osborne et al. 2004) especially those focused on the experience of lone parents (Hinton-Smith 2006, 2007). Hinton-Smith, for example, illustrates the ways in which lone parents in higher education constantly talked about 'balancing' competing responsibilities. Her respondents described the pressures of 'juggling combinations of study, children, paid employment, voluntary work, new relationships and challenging ex-partners' (2006: 10). Among our younger respondents, juggling commitments led to fatigue, but many interviewees also found that part-time jobs frequently clashed with class time and hindered academic performance. This left students with another dilemma:

Well, it was constantly, I mean, it was going to college, I was actually trying to skip classes to go out to get to work to get that, just that extra bit, I mean the money was crap as it was, but still you had to get as much as you could.

(Loretta)

While students from low income families found ways of juggling study with employment, many of them were aware that there were students in their institutions or classes who were privileged to be able to lead a study-focused or even a leisure-focused life. Those leading employment-focused lives had little time to socialize with their more affluent peers, even if they had an inclination to do so. These differences were recognized and sometimes resented (also Little 2006).

A lot of them didn't have jobs and they were all very well off. Like, they could study at night, if you know what I mean.

(Vivian)

They've got more money than you, which makes a big difference about

where they go out. I mean, like, we had a ball here and I couldn't afford to go, and everybody's 'Like, how can you not go to this?'. It's £35 a ticket. You have to buy a dress, everybody's going in these posh dresses.
'Oh you must have at least a cocktail dress.'
'No, I don't really go places wi' cocktails.'
'Well, what do you do when your family are going out?'
'Well, my mum and dad don't go to places where I need a ball-gown.'
So, it's just a different world and I think it's easy for them because they are all together, but it is harder for them to understand your world.

(Ellen)

For some students, these sorts of experience resulted in a clear recognition of the ways in which family resources and cultural capital provided their affluent peers with clear advantages. 'It's just, like, they've just got more money behind them and their parents have been to uni whatever, so they know what they're doing' (Laurie).

Through increased hours, involvement with employers or fellow employees and by being financially dependent upon paid employment, there was clearly a potential for the identity of the respondent to become compromised between that of 'working student' and that of 'student worker'. This in itself could distract from student life, which some recognized in time, but which led to others losing commitment to continued study:

I felt it was creating too much of a distraction from my studies. It was giving me this whole other, like, I was starting to work [in shop] straight after uni when I should have been studying, I was socializing with people from work and I shouldn't have been doing because they are in a sort of different atmosphere to students and they maybe wouldn't appreciate that I would be studying when they were wanting to do things like that.

(Rachel)

Faced with these clear differences in experiences, there was an extent to which working-class students come to prefer social groups comprised of neighbourhood-based peers or new friends that they had met at work. Partly this was a result of a higher level of contact with fellow workers than fellow students, but some clearly felt more comfortable with those who shared a common background and continued to feel ill at ease with more affluent students. And clear differences in the social composition of friendship networks persisted over time – perhaps even becoming more marked as networks became established, resentments built up and the need to work to afford the costs of study reduced contact between social classes.

Conclusion

The experiences of students in higher education have become increasingly diverse and fragmented. Whereas it was once common to think of the main divisions as represented by full- and part-time students or between mature and younger students, the lines of differentiation have become ever more complex. In some respects, a process of differentiation can be welcomed as a move away from a 'one size fits all' model to one that offers the possibility of becoming aligned with the non-linear and reflexive biographies that are the hallmark of late modernity. Yet crucially, the new complexity is perhaps more about class-based processes of stratification than about fresh opportunities. In a previous book we described a process that we referred to as the 'epistemological fallacy of late modernity' (Furlong and Cartmel 1997, 2007) which encompassed the observation that processes of diversification can obscure underlying class divisions, providing the impression of greater equality without providing anything of substance. Changes in higher education have been implemented in such a way that privilege has been protected, partly through harnessing the often rational choices of students with the changes, making persistent inequalities even more obscure.

University life today is very different from university life 40 years ago. Far more people are offered the opportunity of a university education, but there are huge differences in the experience, many of which are unrelated to academic rigour or the distinctiveness of courses but which relate more strongly to processes of social closure (Parkin 1972).

If we recognize that existing funding policies are directly related to processes of stratification, preventing many students from studying away from home, forcing them to juggle intensive engagement with employment with full-time study and effectively blocking cross-class socialization even within courses, then tackling these issues must become a first priority for anyone who professes to support the establishment of a socially just system. Yet through their own conservatism, universities themselves exacerbate problems. Flexible scheduling of lectures, alternative times for all courses, and overcoming the expectation that students must attend most classes could be part of a process of modernization. Contrary to the views held by many lecturers and administrators, students do not simply work for 'beer money' and many have little control over their working hours (and they may have least control at the times of year when exams are scheduled).

The separation between old and new universities (and the more subtle distinctions that mark status within each of these broad categories), result in a class-based set of experiences that ultimately represent clear channels between unequal family origins and unequal labour market positions. Within institutions (especially the older ones), there are also clear divisions between prestigious and less prestigious courses and restricted patterns of interaction between students. There is little evidence that working-class students are becoming absorbed into the assumptive worlds of the established middle classes or developing the sorts of networks that will smooth access to traditional graduate careers.

As Reay and colleagues (2005) have shown, the reproduction of inequalities through higher education is shaped not just by external structures (although financial and admissions policies play a central role) but by the choices made by students themselves as they seek experiences that work within their own comfort zones. University represents a package of experiences which include academic support and stimulation, desired social and cultural encounters and an appropriate fit with external commitments and priorities.

Many of the choices and priorities that underpin processes of differentiation are conditioned by social class, so it is not surprising that the actions of students help reproduce inequalities. The dimension of these processes that tends to be overlooked relates to the active role taken by universities in developing marketing strategies that exploit class-based preferences and insecurities. Essentially, in the case of the established universities, these strategies run directly counter to their professed aim of widening access and help protect their preferred demographic.

5

Changing pathways, altered experiences

The transition to college is no longer marked by a significant transition to adulthood, nor is the college experience itself fully differentiated from work or familial experiences. College students have many choices to make after they enter college. But the numerous enrolment options that are presented by contemporary colleges and universities appear to be embraced by students differently, depending on their social background, and interruptions in contemporary postsecondary schooling are likely to be both involuntary and voluntary . . . Interruptions seem to be more common among students with fewer financial resources and those with lower grades. Thus, students from disadvantaged family backgrounds and those with poorer high school preparation are following pathways in college that are unlikely to lead to the successful completion of degrees.

(Goldrick-Rab 2006: 73)

Introduction

The idea of a higher educational career that involves a whole range of possible pathways from school and through university or college is a relatively new one. The long-held assumption is that students should move rapidly, in a linear fashion, from school-leaving and university entry to graduation. Failure to make swift progress or 'abnormal' patterns of experience have been, and to an extent still are, regarded as indicative of a problematic university career. Indeed, until fairly recently, both researchers and academic administrators used the language of 'continuing' students and 'dropouts': in many ways, the idea of 'failure' and 'dropout' continues to underpin debates about widening access and the student experience. The emergent recognition of the normality of differentiated pathways provides the possibility of a fuller understanding of the ways in which modern students engage with higher education, but also the opportunity to identify the ways in which institutions must change to meet the needs of their new 'customers'. In contexts where young people's lives have become more complex, fragmented and individualized (Furlong and Cartmel 1997), and where educational engagement is portrayed as a lifelong process through which individuals continually revise and upgrade their skills, a dichotomous approach to participation is anachronistic. As the British educational philanthropist Peter Lampl argued 'our obsession with dropouts is a major obstacle to widening access' (2007: 12).

In this chapter we examine the new pathways that define modern contexts of higher education and explore some of the ways in which attempts by institutions of higher education to hold on to past understandings of student engagement are themselves helping to reinforce class-based inequalities: regarding middle-class routes as a benchmark while labelling working-class routes as abnormal or deviant. To do this, we look at the various ways in which differentiated routes are being conceptualized and attempt to assess the extent to which these routes in themselves define class-based modes of participation. We also describe some of the main reasons why today's students are establishing new forms of participation and, in some cases, rejecting the constraints of the traditional model of student.

Progression and survival

'Normal' patterns of student progression tend to be deeply entrenched within institutional cultures. 'Normal' progression is linear although some breaks that occur, as in the case of gap years or time spent studying or gaining skills outside of the home institution, are increasingly regarded as constructive: as enhancing social skills and aiding the development of academic and vocational skills. These institutionally sanctioned breaks effectively endorse long-standing middle-class practices linked to the sponsored cultivation of social capital. This type of 'respectable' break in otherwise linear patterns of progression is far less common among students from working-class families who are more focused on keeping their heads above water financially and academically.

While the majority of students do progress directly through their courses without breaks, those who withdraw at any stage should not automatically be considered to be dropouts nor should the distinction between recreational recesses and constrained intermissions be overlooked. UK statistics show that one in five of those who withdraw from their studies will return the following year (National Audit Office 2007), while others will return at a later stage (occasionally after a break of several years). Moreover, discontinuity should not always be seen in negative terms: those who withdraw may have gained skills during their study period and some will leave due to the promise of better opportunities which may have been secured on the basis of academic or vocational experience. Indeed, Quinn and colleagues argue that most of those who withdraw have solid reasons for doing so and conclude that 'working class students who withdraw early to refocus and re-enter education are real lifelong learners' and suggest that 'institutions and policy-makers have yet to catch up with them' (2005: 68).

In the UK, as in many other countries, the government tends to be interested in overall patterns of completion, expressed in terms of 'survival rates', in which those who fail to complete a course over a specific period of time (which typically allows for a degree of non-linearity) may be labelled as 'dropouts'. However, while higher educational survival rates are regularly published for EU and OECD countries, the statistics are not presented in a way that allows social class-based comparisons. Overall survival rates in the OECD countries in 2004 were 71 per cent, although they vary significantly by country, partly linked to the initial degree of entrance selectivity, but also reflecting patterns of support and social norms regarding patterns of engagement. In Japan, Ireland and the UK, for example, the vast majority of higher educational entrants complete their courses, while completion rates are much lower in France, the USA and Italy (Figure 5.1).

While overall survival rates in the UK are very respectable in comparative terms, there are very strong variations that largely reflect the types of students recruited and forms of stratification in the provision of higher education. In the UK elite institutions, dropout rates are extremely low: the University of Oxford, for example, had a projected dropout rate among

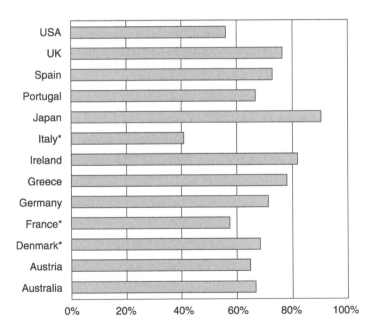

Figure 5.1 Tertiary education survival rates, 2004

Source: OECD (2004, 2006).

Note: *Figures for Denmark, France and Italy relate to 2000.

2004–05 first degree entrants of 1.4 per cent while the University of Bristol predicted a 4 per cent dropout rate (Figure 5.2). At the other end of the scale, the University of Bolton had a projected dropout rate of 31.7 per cent while at Liverpool Hope it was expected to be around 26.3 per cent.

Despite significant changes in the composition of the student body, contemporary survival rates and their variation by institution have changed surprisingly little since the 1950s (although reasons for non-completion have changed somewhat). The Robbins Report (Committee on Higher Education 1963), for example, reported that in 1957 14.3 per cent of undergraduates in arts, science and technology failed to complete their degrees (ranging across universities from 4 per cent to 34 per cent).[1]

Focusing on levels of progression from first to second year of degree courses, the UK National Audit Office (2007) shows the extent to which continuation rates today vary by the status of institutions. Overall, around 91.6 per cent of students who start the first year of a degree course continue to second year. Against this overall average, more than 95 per cent continue from first to second year in the elite Russell Group institutions, compared to around 89 per cent in the post-1992 universities. Standard deviations are also much higher in post-1992 institutions. Subjects studied are also important: subjects such as medicine and dentistry have relatively high rates of continuity (98 per cent) while combined studies has one of the lowest retention rates (83 per cent).

In essence, rates of continuity between first and second year reflect the advantages of the different groups of students recruited to various courses and institutions. Those who enter with three A grades at A level are far more likely to continue than those with two D grades at A level, while compared to

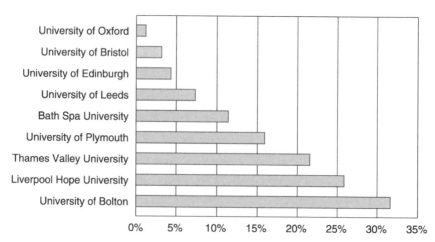

Figure 5.2 Projected dropout rates among students starting a first degree in 2004–05 at various institutions

Source: National Audit Office (2007).

those from middle-class families, students from the working classes are less likely to continue (National Audit Office 2007). In terms of first year to second year continuity, overall, just four factors explain 70 per cent of the variance between institutions: recruitment skewed towards those from neighbourhoods with high rates of participation (which can be regarded as a proxy for middle-class membership); recruiting students with strong qualification profiles (another middle-class proxy); admitting relatively small numbers of mature students (who often lack traditional qualifications); and offering a portfolio of courses that include subjects such as medicine and dentistry (which overwhelmingly recruit from the middle classes) (National Audit Office 2007).

Although expressed in more cautious, politically neutral terms by the National Audit Office, continuity between first and second year of study is powerfully affected by social class-related variables with working-class students being the clear losers. With the status hierarchy of institutions clearly reflecting the class composition of the student body, institutions can be used as a rough proxy for social class and statistics show very clearly that those universities and colleges in which working-class students are most strongly represented are those that consistently have the highest rates of non-completion. While such evidence supports the claim that institutional arrangements help reproduce class-based advantage, we must also be aware that some students in new universities may be weak academically and recognize that entry qualifications have a much more direct bearing on rates of completion. While more elusive, evidence of a direct casual link between social class and patterns of completion has emerged from a number of studies. In the UK, Smith and Naylor (2001) used evidence collected from around 400,000 students leaving pre-1992 universities to show that students from the least advantaged social classes were significantly over-represented among the non-completers. Similarly in the USA, Goldrick-Rab showed that interrupted modes of attendance were most common among low SES students, 'not because they are shopping, partying, or choosing to take time off to "find themselves" but because they have suffered academically or financially in school' (2006: 73). Indeed, Goldrick-Rab argues that complex pathways through higher education have become commonplace with around half of all US undergraduates changing institution at some stage and around a third breaking their studies to take time out.

In the West of Scotland survey, non-linear patterns of progression were extremely common, but these breaks tended to be reactions (chosen, or more typically enforced) to adverse financial, academic or social circumstances. Again, breaks were often temporary and many of those who took time out expressed an intention, or a desire, to return at a later stage. Among members of the West of Scotland cohort who had entered higher education, seven different routes could be identified:

• Linear, continuous education pathways in which young people had entered university or college directly and progressed without a break.

- Repeaters who had re-taken a year of study in the same course.
- Restarts who had left one course or institution to enter a different institution or begin a different course at the same college or university.
- Deferrers who worked for a year or more before returning to education.
- Progressers who completed one course and moved on to another, more advanced course, without entering the labour market.
- Dropouts who left a course without completing and who had not enrolled in a further course.
- Returners who after dropping out or completing a short course (e.g. HNC/HND) entered employment before returning to higher education.

Among these less advantaged students, breaks were frequently linked to the need to find employment to get their finances back in order, were enforced due to failing courses or on occasions linked to the need to care or provide for the family. In other words, non-linear forms of progression can be found among both middle-class and working-class students, but the former can typically be regarded as a recreational recess while the latter tends to be a constrained intermission.

> I did like being at university. I liked the people and that. I enjoyed the course. I thought it was really good, but at the end of the day it just got back to money again. That was the thing that was going to stop me.
>
> (Flora)

Integration and non-completion

Non-completion has long been a concern to institutions and, in England, the minds of university administrators have become more focused on rates of completion since the government started publishing 'league tables' detailing survival rates alongside benchmarks (which take account of characteristics of student intake) that institutions are expected to meet in order to satisfy the Office of Fair Access. In terms of understanding reasons for non-completion, one widely accepted explanation relates to the extent to which students are successfully integrated in the institution. Tinto (1975, 1987, 1993), for example, has been influential in arguing that patterns of non-completion can largely be explained by a lack of academic and social integration within universities and colleges. Those who 'drop out' of university tend to be poorly integrated, isolated, and may 'perceive themselves as being substantially at odds with the institution' (Tinto 1987: 53).

As Tinto recognized, integration could be affected by characteristics of the institution and its policies and ethos, but is also strongly affected by socio-economic background. Thus, he argues that 'college persisters are more likely to come from families whose parents are more educated, are more urbane and more affluent' (1975: 100). This position is supported by a wide range of studies that demonstrate the extent to which working-class students often have a peripheral attachment to their institutions, with course work competing for time with a range of other pressing commitments, particularly employment. There is also evidence suggesting that working-class students have weaker peer support networks (Harvey and Drew 2006).

Although patterns of integration are affected as much by factors external to the institution as by internal arrangements, Tinto's ideas have prompted many institutions to consider ways in which they can intervene to promote higher levels of integration among non-traditional and less advantaged students. Here the recently introduced National Student Satisfaction Surveys can be used not just as a measure of consumer endorsement of the 'products' provided by institutions, but also as an indicator of patterns of integration. However, to be used in this way, it is necessary to move beyond descriptive summaries of patterns of satisfaction at the level of the institution or course and engage in a more detailed analysis that identifies variation by a range of other background factors, such as social class and prior attainment. While this type of research has not been undertaken nationally on a systematic basis, many studies have been carried out by individual institutions. In a study conducted at Middlesex University, for example, patterns of retention were clearly linked to integration and satisfaction (Harvey and Drew 2006). The Middlesex study found that poor integration could be linked to weak involvement with fellow students, dissatisfaction with accommodation and general feelings that social and academic support was not readily available. Patterns of retention were also linked to academic dissatisfaction, failure and detachment (Harvey and Drew 2006).

Clearly there are a wide range of factors that are associated with student retention. Internal factors associated with 'non-completion' include institutional and course specific factors which may see students on courses or at universities that they come to regard as poor choices, as difficult to cope with academically or as socially alienating. Indeed, for students who fail to complete a course, disappointment with the course and the recognition that a poor choice had been made tend to be among the main reasons given for quitting a course (Rickinson and Rutherford 1995; Baird 2002; Harvey and Drew 2006). When students encounter difficulties or become disillusioned, universities and colleges are not always proactive in suggesting course changes, time out or switching to a part-time mode of study, and university careers services tend not to concern themselves with identifying career opportunities for early leavers (Quinn et al. 2005). In the UK, a high proportion of those who see themselves as having made a poor choice of course were allocated their places during the 'clearing' process (Davies and Elias 2003) under which potential students who have not been accepted for their first choice courses are able to apply for courses with spare capacity. It has also been claimed that careers officers and teachers often push working-class males towards class-stereotyped subjects without due regard for their interests (Quinn et al. 2005).

In a recent report on student retention, the National Audit Office (2007) listed a range of (overlapping) reasons frequently given for withdrawing from a course. These included: personal reasons such as illness or difficulties

in balancing obligations; a lack of integration such as problems fitting in
socially or failing to establish a 'bond' with the institution; dissatisfaction
with the course, institution or standard of teaching; a lack of preparation
such as the failure to develop appropriate study skills or experiencing
difficulties coping with the demands of the course; making the wrong choice
of course sometimes linked to a lack of clear information about courses or
institutions; financial reasons often linked to debt, fear of debt and difficulties combining study with extensive employment commitments; and leaving
to take up more attractive opportunities. Yet, as noted by Yorke and Longden
(2008), withdrawal is rarely triggered by a single factor but tends to be linked
to a combination of factors. In the West of Scotland study, there were
examples of students who had left a course for each of the reasons identified
by the National Audit Office. However, among these less advantaged
students, financial issues and problems relating to lack of integration were
most common.

> I didn't like being a student at all . . . I couldn't put my finger on any one
> thing, it's just wee bits. I didn't like the studying, I didn't like the not
> having enough money all the time, didn't like, I don't know . . . However,
> I liked the college itself and I liked the people that were there, I just
> didn't like the lifestyle . . . I just got offered that job as a rough-caster
> and I just took it . . . More money . . . I don't like sitting about, I don't
> like office jobs or anything like that, I prefer being out, out in the open.
>
> (Sammy)

> Aye they were nice, but different just . . . I don't think I was very studenty
> and they were more studenty like, I don't know, I just don't think I
> fitted in.
>
> (Jean)

In a variety of ways linked to the organization of higher educational institutions, student expectations are frequently not met. Some of the reasons
relate to the ways in which courses are delivered, the approaches of teaching
and administrative staff, the backgrounds of fellow students, accommodation
or geographical accessibility. For non-traditional students, these issues can
be more problematic simply because their expectations are less likely to be
guided by the experiences of others they know who have been through
higher education. As Harvey and Drew note, first generation students tend
to expect higher levels of support than they actually experience. 'First generation students are likely to find that their presumptions about the higher
education experience are not met, especially around the availability of teaching staff, which can affect their persistence and performance' (2006: 53).

There is also evidence that less advantaged and non-traditional students
can feel isolated and may feel that they have little in common with their
peers. This is especially true in traditional and elite institutions (Bowl 2003;
Forsyth and Furlong 2003). Related to this, Christie and colleagues (2005)
have argued that an important distinction can be made between what they

refer to as 'day students' and their peers who enjoy a traditional, all-embracing, university experience. 'Day students' regard higher education as an activity similar to traditional employment: as something that they engage in between the hours of 9 and 5 and as a set of activities largely separated from those that characterize their ordinary lives. The 'privatized worker' identified by Goldthorpe and colleagues (1969), who largely left their employment-based identities at the factory gates, has a clear parallel in the modern university. Being a student is not necessarily regarded as central to the overall identities of working-class students. In these circumstances, study may be regarded as 'an extension to their existing lives rather than as a complete break from it' (Christie et al. 2005: 12). Yet students who live parallel lives in education and employment can experience a range of conflicts that compromise emerging identities. In particular, peer groups may act in ways that serve to reinforce a worker identity at the expense of a student identity, with repercussions for educational careers.

For Christie and colleagues (2005), student identities can be regarded as negotiated outcomes in which the student considers the desirability of different forms of integration, reflects on the advantages and disadvantages of different levels of engagement and assesses the extent to which student life can be accommodated within the matrix of competing interests and commitments (also Ball et al. 2000). Christie and colleagues describe the highly integrated students as the 'absorbed' and suggest that activities and relationships linked to the university tend to be privileged. A notable feature of the students in the 'absorbed' group was the importance they attached to fitting in to social networks at university. As such, they viewed being a 'day' student as a distinct disadvantage, because it was much more difficult to become embedded in university-based friendship networks (2005: 14). Such feelings were also evident among the West of Scotland respondents.

> There is a small group that I get on well with, but in general they have very different backgrounds to me and it makes it quite difficult. They have also got a lot more money which means you can't really socialize with them in the same way.
>
> (Heather)

These observations about the embedded student identities of those from middle-class families compared to the detached identities of non-traditional students were explored by Bourdieu (1996) who drew attention to the ways in which the cultural capital of the middle classes provided powerful advantages in educational institutions based on middle-class values. Middle-class students tend to fit into university very easily, the assumptions and expectations of academic staff and fellow students represent a continuity of the cultural worlds of the family. As Bourdieu and Wacquant note, they encounter 'a social world of which it is a product, it is like a "fish in water": it does not feel the weight of the water and it takes the world about itself for granted' (1992: 127, quoted in Curtis 2007). In contrast, the isolation of working-class students was viewed as inevitable given the powerful differences in habitus.

Bourdieu described working-class students in elite institutions as 'cultural outsiders' and argued that disadvantaged students often found themselves in a state of 'double isolation', unable to fit into the culture of the institution yet becoming increasingly uncomfortable in the working-class home and community environment (1996: 107).

Clearly there are institutional issues that need to be addressed so that working-class students come to regard themselves as fully integrated, 'absorbed' (Christie et al. 2005), students who participate on an equal basis to that of their more advantaged peers. But many of the most powerful barriers to integration relate to factors external to the institution. While it is true that working-class students can lack confidence, can have difficulties in adjusting to university life and are often less sure of the long-term benefits of higher education, there are also significant resource issues that impact on the student experience. Families are often not in a position to provide financial aid and they often lack the means of cushioning their offspring if they encounter the sort of crisis points that more affluent students can largely take in their stride. Working-class students are also more likely to have to juggle study with long hours in employment which can lead to exhaustion, disillusionment and poor marks.

In this context, universities have been described as 'greedy institutions' that make such heavy and inflexible demands on the time of students (assuming they will prioritize their studies over all other competing activities, such as employment and childcare) that participants who lack the resources to allow the university to take centre stage will inevitably struggle to keep up (Acker 1980; Edwards 1993; Hinton-Smith 2007). Thus, the excessive and insatiable demands that the institutions make on the time of their students inevitably put those groups with limited time (such as working students and students with family responsibilities) at a disadvantage. In this context, students in the West of Scotland survey frequently highlighted the difficulties students faced combining full-time study with long working hours and extensive travel, illustrating the conflicts between the demands of their college and the demands of their employers (see Chapter 4). For some students, this discord between inflexible study arrangements and unaccommodating employers can contribute to early withdrawal (Callender and Kemp 2000). For those who continue, the way in which the curriculum is organized can have a powerful impact on patterns of (academic and non-academic) interaction with fellow students and staff (Brennan and Osborne 2008).

While universities have traditionally been 'greedy institutions', demanding the full attention of their students, the situation has only become problematic because of inadequate funding arrangements under which those who lack substantial family support are unable to satisfy the demands of the institution. Moreover, to perform well at university, students are not simply required to devote a set amount of time to a given piece of work, but should devote whatever time is necessary to produce academic work that they feel does full justice to their abilities, however long that might take. Under such conditions, those without significant competing demands on their time have considerable advantages and are likely to outperform those with less control over their time.

New modes of engagement

If a lack of institutional integration is central to an understanding of patterns of survival in higher education, then it is important that we look more closely at the bonds that exist between students and their colleges and universities. It has been argued, for example, that in modern, mass contexts, students are often relatively disengaged and satisfactions derive not so much from academic stimulation but from the social context of the institution.

Describing modern students as 'reluctant intellectuals', Côté and Allahar (2007) argue that contemporary students are not engaged in academic life in a traditional sense in which intellectual curiosity acts as a prime driver, but cut corners wherever possible and expect to obtain 'good' degrees with minimal effort. While placing a large part of the blame on grade inflation in (North American) high schools and collusion by universities who seek to placate poor students with high grade expectations, Côté and Allahar argue that university peer groups no longer value academic intellectual achievement. Based on Canadian evidence, they argue that those in the top 10 per cent in terms of achievement are frequently marginalized by peers, while a further 20 per cent make no attempt to improve their grades so as not to risk being stigmatized as swots or intellectuals.

Whereas a series of national surveys of student satisfaction has recently been introduced in the UK, in Canada and the USA attempts are made to monitor patterns of disengagement. Summarizing the general picture, Côté and Allahar argue that these surveys tend to show that around one in ten can be described as 'fully engaged' in that that they fulfil the work expectations of their teachers. Around four in ten are described as 'partially engaged', doing less work than expected of them, but sufficient to avoid complaints or failure. Yet between 40 and 50 per cent are regarded as 'disengaged', doing either nothing or as little work as possible. Based on a survey of faculty at the University of Western Ontario, Côté and Allahar found that three in four staff judged no more than 10 per cent of their students as 'top notch' while a third thought that less than one in ten were fully engaged. Nevertheless, almost one in two thought that, compared to past practice, students were getting higher grades for either the same or less effort. According to Côté and Allahar, patterns of involvement are directly affected by their observations of peers and by their desire to 'fit in'. It is also suggested that class work is prioritized and time allocated is weighted in the light of other commitments and pressures, especially those linked to employment.

While there is a lack of UK data on patterns of student engagement or of lecturers' assessment of ability, effort or grade inflation, it would be surprising if the UK experience was radically different. Indeed, in North

America and the UK, we might want to ask why survival rates are so high if students are so lacking in intellectual engagement. It is likely that completion rates are affected by instrumentalism and that some of the more significant incentives for continued participation are related to labour market incentives rather than to intrinsic academic rewards.

In a small-scale study in the south-west of England, Brooks (2007) studied the different ways in which students invested in campus culture and investigated approaches to learning. She identified four approaches to learning which she referred to as 'active', 'passive', 'slacker' and 'consumerist'. Whereas students adopting active approaches to learning can be seen as fully engaged in a traditional sense, the 'consumerist' approach represents an adaptation to the comodification of learning with students as consumers of a product expecting to get their money's worth. The 'passsive' and 'slacker' approaches represent different forms of disengagement. The former tend to turn up for lectures and seminars but are unlikely to prepare or participate in discussion. In the words of one of Brooks' 'passives', 'In seminars I'm a passive student, I just don't get it, so when she asks a question I do just sit there with a blank expression on my face' (Brooks 2007). In contrast, the slackers were proud of their ability to play the system, to get by with minimum effort and to enjoy a student life that was leisure focused rather than academically focused.

As a small-scale qualitative study conducted in a single institution, it would be wrong to attempt to use Brooks' work as a basis for quantifying student approaches to learning. Indeed, despite concerns about levels of disengagement and instrumentalism, the best evidence available suggests that modern UK students are engaged and largely satisfied with their experience of higher education. The 2007 National Student Survey (HEFCE 2007), for example, received responses from 177,000 students with 81 per cent expressing overall satisfaction with their experience at college or university. While there were differences between institutions, these were relatively small: among the mainstream universities ranging from 95 per cent at the Open University to 70 per cent at London Metropolitan University. Of the 146 institutions represented, just 18 registered overall satisfaction scores of less than 75 per cent while eight had scores of more than 90 per cent. The large majority of students were also satisfied with the quality of teaching on their course (82 per cent), with the academic support provided (71 per cent), with the organization and management of their college or university (71 per cent), with the learning resources made available (80 per cent) and with opportunities for personal development (77 per cent). Levels of satisfaction with assessment and feedback arrangements were slightly lower (61 per cent), perhaps reflecting disappointment with grades (HEFCE 2007).

While a course can meet expectations and while students can express high levels of satisfaction with their courses, it is possible that positive feelings towards the institution may reflect an undemanding workload and high pass rates in return for minimal effort. In other words, if institutional and individual expectations are aligned within a low demand equilibrium, students may be under-stretched, but satisfied. The National Student Survey does not facilitate further exploration of these issues nor does it currently permit an analysis based on social class.

Information from the (nationally representative) Scottish School Leavers Surveys suggests that students display both high levels of instrumentalism at the same time as being engaged with their chosen subject. Among respondents who were aged 24 in 2004, 89 per cent said that they attended university or college because they were particularly interested in a particular subject while just over a third (36 per cent) progressed to higher education as they saw it as a natural next step after school (Biggart et al. 2005). While interested in their chosen subject, the vast majority were influenced by the perceived benefits of higher education on their future careers. More than nine in ten (91 per cent) indicated that they undertook higher education so that they would get a more satisfying job in the future while 86 per cent expected it to lead to a better-paid job in the future.

Figures from the West of Scotland Survey of young people from less advantaged families also highlight the complexity of motives for engaging in higher education. These students also placed a strong emphasis on the career benefits of higher education with 93 per cent indicating that the perceived link between qualifications and good jobs influenced decisions about progression. Higher education was also thought of as representing a natural progression, backed up with some pressure from parents. Almost three in ten (27 per cent) said that their parents wanted them to go while one in four (25 per cent) thought that it is what they should be doing at their age and 15 per cent said that they had no idea what else to do. A significant number progressed because of a perceived lack of jobs in their locality (15 per cent), because it was seen as being an easier life than the alternatives (9 per cent) or because it helped them leave home or move out of the area where they lived (20 per cent) (but double that (42 per cent) in rural areas like Argyll where university has long been regarded as providing the best opportunity to establish a new, non-rural life) (Forsyth and Furlong 2000, 2003).

In many respects, an increase in the cultural diversity of intakes to higher education will inevitably be reflected in a greater variety of motives for higher study and a wider range of approaches to accommodating study and other core activities such as work and leisure. Interestingly, among members of the West of Scotland sample who progressed to higher education, only 3 per cent strongly agreed with the view that higher education is only for 'really clever people' while two-thirds (66 per cent) disagreed with the proposition. In a sense, these views represent an essential underpinning of the wider access agenda: the idea that potential is limited by ability is not a proposition that finds widespread support among the upper classes but is one that has traditionally framed the educational aspirations of the working classes. To go back to Côté and Allahar's lament about declining standards and poor levels of engagement, evidence about motives for participation suggest that for many students the idea that higher education is about

intellectual exploration and engagement is somewhat dated, perhaps necessarily so. There are parallels here between the 'massification' of higher
education and the raising of the school-leaving age to 16 in 1972, a process
which had a dramatic effect on the social composition of the upper
secondary school which eventually led to a revision of teacher expectations
and changes in the curriculum (Biggart and Furlong 1996). University and
college lecturers have yet to come to terms with these changes by accepting
that many of their future students will lack an intrinsic interest in their
subject and regard university instrumentally. In this context, describing how
he would sell university to others in his neighbourhood, one of the West
of Scotland respondents stressed the importance of speaking to them in a
language they understood:

> Say there is hundreds of birds up there, know what I mean. It is a good
> experience, it gets you out of here, get student loans, massive amounts
> of money, as long as you do some studying you get hundreds of time to
> kick about, get steaming. Basically do everything you do now, do a bit of
> studying and you will end up with a degree one day.
>
> (Jock)

Conclusion

As the numbers of people experiencing higher education increase, the
diversity of routes through higher education is also likely to grow. Student
experiences will increasing be fragmented and non-linear, characterized by
breaks and changes of direction. While complex higher educational careers
are not necessarily problematic, it is clear that institutions need to do more
to accommodate change while the government's preoccupation with 'dropouts' shows a failure to engage with the environment within which young
people live their lives (partly created, of course, by policies towards student
finance). In many respects, modern (non-linear) forms of engagement
involve an increased representation of 'non-traditional' (i.e. working-class)
students who lack the resources to follow 'traditional' routes. To ensure that
such routes are not associated with disadvantage, the 'greediness' of higher
education institutions has to be curbed. Without such a curb on their
appetite there will inevitably be conflicts with the social justice agenda.

One of the difficult questions that needs to be resolved relates to how
institutions should involve students and ensure their effective integration
into a learning community without making presumptions about the ways in
which students should prioritize their activities. A forward-looking institution perhaps needs to allow students the scope to manage their own diaries,
to choose which learning activities they value most, avoiding the temptation
to penalize students who decide to skip lectures or tutorials and providing
alternative means of delivery for those who find it difficult to attend regularly. But while integration remains desirable, it is important to recognize

that some will wish to complete a degree without taking on the identity of student in any meaningful way.

Recognizing the importance of creating diverse environments that suit the needs of a wide variety of learners inevitably means abandoning the label 'dropout' and moving away from a system that 'names and shames' those institutions in which a relatively high proportion of students fail to complete within a set time frame. Under the current system, those institutions that show a real commitment to wider access and who make opportunities available to those who lack 'traditional' entry qualifications are being penalized for their efforts, while universities who, by playing it safe, effectively subvert the social justice agenda are rewarded.

While many academics would be happy to endorse the idea of diverse higher educational experiences, one of the more controversial aspects of a mass system of higher education centres on the motivation and intellectual engagement of the new student body. In the modern labour market, higher educational credentials have become increasingly necessary for those wishing to access a wide range of careers and it is inevitable that some students will regard their degrees as a means to an end rather than reflecting a deep interest in a subject. Although most students do have some interest in the subjects they study, it is important for academics to avoid elitist approaches to engagement. Moreover, it is important that we recognize that higher education is not just about formal learning and academic engagement. For young people it is also about independence and becoming an adult and about lifestyle and sexual freedom. Universities should not expect to take centre stage in the lifecourse of young adults or demand that students' commitment transcends the instrumental.

6

Differential rewards

While it is certainly true that attendance at 'pre-92' universities generally bestows an employment advantage, the extent of the advantage is
mediated by factors such as the subject studied and the background
characteristics of the graduates. For some groups of students, attending
a 'pre-92' university may bestow little employment advantage. And when
the effects of factors such as institution attended, subject studied, entry
qualifications and degree classifications are controlled for, graduates
from disadvantaged groups still appear to do less well than other
students on several employment criteria.

(Brennan and Shah 2003: 40)

Introduction

Without suggesting that potential students engage in a process of fully
conscious, rational, economic planning, the decision to follow a course of
higher education, foregoing earnings and accumulating debt, does tend to
be influenced by perceptions of future gains. Graduates have lower rates of
unemployment and their average lifetime earnings are significantly higher
than those of peers who have made earlier exits from the educational system.
Indeed, as discussed in Chapter 3, the political justification for passing an
increasing proportion of the costs of study to the student and their families is
linked to the understanding that the individual participant is a key
beneficiary.

While it is true that higher education can be considered to be an investment that brings long-term career benefits, the supply of graduates has
grown significantly over the past two decades and further increases are being
encouraged by government. To maintain the traditional graduate career
premium, it is necessary to have a corresponding growth in the number of
professional, managerial and highly skilled positions in the labour market to
absorb the increased flow of qualified labour. Otherwise there is the risk that

an increased supply of graduates will simply lead to a process of qualification inflation resulting in the emergence of an under-employed and indebted graduate workforce locked into the precarious fringes of the economy.

With experiences of higher education being highly stratified, the graduate population is segmented with some groups channelled towards prestigious and highly rewarding careers while others follow routes into routine forms of employment or to jobs only recently accepted as appropriate for graduates. In this chapter we explore changes in the graduate labour market and in transitions from higher education to employment. We also examine the barriers that block mobility and help maintain divisions in the labour market and consider the benefits of higher education by looking at patterns of debt and reward and at students' own evaluations of the gains associated with extended educational participation.

The changing graduate labour market

In her book, *Class Practices,* Fiona Devine (2004) reflects on the relationship between changing labour market opportunities and processes of social reproduction. While generational transfers of advantage between elite groups may be relatively unaffected by the changes, she suggests that, for the middle classes, it has become more difficult to transfer class advantage. The parents of the young people entering university today benefited from a significant expansion of professional and managerial opportunities and were frequently able to secure middle-class careers without the need to obtain a degree. A process of qualification inflation, together with more limited growth, or even stagnation, of opportunities for employment in the professional and managerial sector means not only that degrees are required to enter a growing range of jobs, but also that degrees have become a devalued currency which no longer guarantee privileged opportunities. As Saunders reminds us, 'higher education is a classic "positional good" – the more people have it, the less valuable it becomes as a means to entering top positions, but the greater is the penalty for those who fail to get access' (1996: 81).

Heath and Payne (2000) show that of those born between 1950 and 1959 (of whom many will be parents of current undergraduates and recent graduates), around 42 per cent of males and 37 per cent of females found employment in professional and managerial occupations. Yet among this age group, the numbers entering university represented around 6 per cent of the cohort (Blanden and Machin 2004). Today more than four in ten enter higher education (around five in ten in Scotland) yet less than three in ten employees work in professional and managerial occupations (classes I and II) (Self and Zealey 2007). Higher education has become a prerequisite for entry into high-level employment, but no longer offers guarantees.

Indeed, while Goldthorpe and colleagues (1980) explained the increase in social mobility in the post-war period as being triggered by 'room at the top' (referring to the large increase in professional and managerial positions, especially within the expanding public service organizations), more recent research has shown that absolute chances of mobility have declined since around 1980 (Goldthorpe and Mills 2000). For young people and their parents, these changes result in significant pressures: parents are concerned that their children enjoy a lifestyle similar to their own while young people are aware of the need to jump academic hurdles (irrespective of aptitude or interest) in order to secure reasonable employment prospects.

The effective reproduction of advantage requires substantial investment on the part of young people and their parents and resource transfers between generations are substantial (Swartz and O'Brien 2009). With an extension of dependency and a reduction in state support in the USA and in Europe, an increasing proportion of the costs of child-rearing are incurred during young adulthood (Swartz and O'Brien 2009). Significant class-based differences in the levels of resource transfer mean that parental subsidies have an important impact on processes of social reproduction.

With the ratio of employment opportunities within the traditional gradu-ate sector (corresponding to social classes I and II) to the number of young people completing high education being unfavourable, there is a danger that university will come to be regarded as a risky investment, especially for families with limited resources. Indeed, if we continue to define the graduate labour market in a traditional, narrow way we have to be clear that most graduates will never manage to work in this sector. Yet in a contemporary context we can perhaps define graduate employment as being those forms of employment that current graduates are likely to enter and recognize that some forms of employment will bear little resemblance to traditional forms of graduate work. The term graduate employment has in fact come to be interpreted much more widely, encompassing some forms of employment that are still dominated by non-graduates. Effectively the graduate labour market has become segmented into secure and less secure zones as well as into segments that have a looser correspondence to what may be thought of as graduate skills.

Recognizing these divisions, Purcell and colleagues (2004) make a distinc-tion between four types of graduate employment: traditional, modern, new and niche (Table 6.1). Whereas traditional graduate jobs have long been the more or less exclusive preserve of those with university degrees (such as lawyers, doctors and scientists), the other three sectors of the graduate labour market refer to those areas that have gradually become (or are still becoming) dominated by workers with degrees; a process that can be linked to the growth of higher education over the past two decades or so and which may be interpreted as an indicator of qualification inflation. Modern gradu-ate jobs relate to newer professions and to those areas of employment where graduate status started to become required in the 1980s (such as journalism and accountancy). New graduate jobs refer to those sectors of employment that have more recently begun to focus on graduate recruitment (such as marketing and physiotherapy) while niche occupations are those where a

Table 6.1 Purcell et al.'s Classification of Graduate Occupations

Type of occupation	Description	Examples
Traditional graduate occupations	The established professions for which, historically, the normal route has been via an undergraduate degree programme	Solicitors Medical practitioners HE, FE and secondary education teachers Biological scientists/biochemists
Modern graduate occupations	The newer professions, particularly in management, IT and creative vocational areas, which graduates have been entering increasingly since the 1980s	Charted and certified accountants Software engineers, computer programmers Authors/writers/journalists
New graduate occupations	Areas of employment to which graduates have increasingly been recruited in large numbers; mainly new administrative, technical and 'caring' occupations	Marketing and sales, advertising managers Physiotherapists, occupational hygienists Social workers, probation, welfare officers Clothing designers
Niche graduate occupations	Occupations where the majority of incumbents are not graduates, but within which there are stable or growing specialist *niches* which require higher education skills and knowledge	Entertainment and sports managers Hotel, accommodation managers Midwives Buyers (non-retail)
Non-graduate occupations	Graduates are also found in jobs that are likely to constitute under-utilization of their higher education skills and knowledge	Sales assistants Filing and record clerks Routine laboratory testers Debt, rent and cash collectors

Source: Purcell et al. (2004: 6).

minority of incumbents are graduates but in which there are growing specialist niches where graduates are employed (hotel managers and buyers).

Purcell and her colleagues (2005) traced the early careers of 8,600 graduates from a representative sample of 38 higher education institutes in 1999. Over a four-year period they found considerable career movement with employment positions tending to improve substantially over time. Immediately after graduation, around two-thirds were in employment, although almost half of these were in non-graduate forms of employment.

Sixteen per cent were unemployed immediately after graduating, with one in four encountering a period of unemployment at some time during their first four years in the labour market. Yet over time there was clear movement away from non-graduate forms of employment to graduate careers. Four years after graduation, 19 per cent of their sample were in traditional graduate occupations, 20 per cent in modern graduate occupations, 22 per cent in new graduate occupations and 21 per cent in niche graduate employment. Just 17 per cent were in non-graduate forms of employment.

Transitions

For graduates, as well as for those who enter the labour market directly from school, routes between education and work have become protracted and increasingly complex. It is more difficult to move directly into stable forms of employment and many have fragmented, non-linear transitions in which they combine study and work, take up temporary forms of employment and encounter periods of unemployment or under-employment. To an extent, non-linear transitions are most common among those with relatively poor qualifications, those who leave education at an early stage and those who live in economically depressed areas (Furlong et al. 2003). Yet as discussed in Chapter 4, for some, experiences of higher education will be characterized by non-linearity. Others will face a fragmented set of experiences following graduation and may live out their careers in the precarious sectors of the labour market.

The speed and smoothness of the transition from higher education to graduate jobs or to relatively stable forms of employment are affected by a range of factors including the state of the local labour market, the willingness and ability of graduates to seek jobs nationally, the types of course followed, the institution attended and by flexibility about the sorts of employment considered acceptable. Some may be willing, or able, to hold out until the 'right' job comes along; others may have little alternative but to take up the first opportunity, regardless of pay, status or aspiration.

As a result of scarcity and vocational relevance, rapid entry to full-time permanent jobs following graduation is slightly more common among those who take medical and related courses as well as engineering, business studies, education and law (Pearson et al. 2000; Furlong and Cartmel 2005; Purcell et al. 2005). In contrast, rates of entry to graduate jobs tend to be lower in arts, humanities, languages, social sciences and maths, computing and natural sciences. There is also evidence that working-class graduates and females find it more difficult to secure graduate employment, although to an extent, for working-class graduates, potential handicaps are reduced on account of their over-representation on vocational courses, some of which have clear routes to employment (Furlong and Cartmel 2005).

Young people's progress from college and university into the labour market, and, in particular, the graduate sectors of the labour market is often slow

(Furlong and Cartmel 2005; Purcell et al. 2005). As such, attempts to assess the benefits of higher education through the use of outcome data collected in the months following graduation (as is the practice for many destination surveys) are likely to yield pessimistic results. Among the West of Scotland sample, a month after leaving higher education, only around a third of graduates had full-time permanent jobs and many of these were not in forms of employment usually reserved for graduates. At age 22, just over four in ten higher education participants had entered a (broadly defined) graduate occupation with just one in five employed in what was defined as a relatively secure graduate position. Levels of unemployment immediately after leaving college or university were extremely high, although it tended to be a fleeting experience and extended or repeated unemployment was rare (Furlong and Cartmel 2005). While these figures relate to a sample of students from less advantaged families, statistics compiled by the Higher Education Statistics Agency (HESA) are quite similar: in December 2004, 38 per cent of students who had entered the labour market were in non-graduate employment six months after completing their degrees (*Guardian* 2005). The figures are not surprising given the imbalance between supply and demand. Using figures from 2001, Brown and colleagues (2003) argued that in excess of 300,000 graduates were competing for less than 15,000 'elite jobs', many with 'blue chip' companies offering relatively poor starting salaries. The slow start to graduate careers and associated frustration was frequently highlighted by West of Scotland respondents:

It is happening a little slower than I expected, but I'm doing two jobs at the moment and hoping to get access to the graduate trainee scheme in social work in the next year or two.

(Mary)

It seems to be getting better as I get older and gain experience, although I wish it would happen faster.

(Craig)

On the surface, the picture does not look encouraging, yet the situation is not as depressing as it seems. Although progress towards graduate jobs is slow, progress does occur and longitudinal work clearly shows increases in the number of graduates employed in positions requiring advanced qualifications as time goes by (Purcell et al. 2005). Figures from the Higher Education Statistics Agency (2007a), for example, show that three and a half years after graduation, around eight in ten will be employed in graduate jobs. Purcell and colleagues (2005) show that while around one in two graduates began their careers in non-graduate jobs, seven years after graduation only 15 per cent were still in non-graduate forms of employment. Internationally, transitions from higher education to employment in the UK are relatively favourable. Around 8 per cent spend the first four years after graduation mainly in short-term employment while just 2 per cent are mainly unemployed, compared to a European average of 13 and 5 per cent respectively (Teichler 2007). In the Netherlands, Germany, Austria, France, Spain and Italy, more than one in ten spent their first four post-graduation years mostly in short-term jobs (Teichler 2007).

Early snapshots of occupational position are misleading for two reasons. First, because the boundaries between graduate and non-graduate jobs can be 'fuzzy' (Keep 2004) as university leavers take low-skilled temporary jobs while searching for positions that they regard as more appropriate. Second, because early insecurity is often part of the 'normal' career trajectories in some graduate occupations.

On leaving higher education, young people find themselves in various degrees of proximity to the labour market. A few will have well-developed plans and explicit career strategies. They may have learnt about potential careers and of the ways in which recruitment is organized; they may even have approached potential employers before leaving university. Some of those who have followed vocational courses will already know something about opportunities and methods of securing careers within their area of learning, and some will have a clear idea about their next move. Those who have followed general degree courses may be less well prepared and their career plans may be undeveloped or non-existent. For many, the period immediately following the completion of their course represents a moratorium in which they reflect and attempt to develop a career strategy or think about their next moves or even take an extended holiday.

The 'fuzzy' boundaries between non-graduate and non-graduate jobs arise because many will need a job of some sort to support a moratorium and a high proportion of new graduates will remain in the job they used to support their studies. In the West of Scotland sample, eight in ten students held part-time jobs while studying and more than six in ten retained these same jobs following graduation. As such, the end of higher education did not necessarily lead to an abrupt transition from one main activity (education) to another (a new job or unemployment). While graduation tended to be accompanied by an intensification of job search activity, many began the search for graduate jobs while continuing to work in the jobs that they had held during their time at university or college and even increased the hours worked in their temporary job to occupy the time that was once filled by study. For many, these jobs helped them meet their financial commitments, maintain leisure and consumption lifestyles and pay the rent while they looked for jobs that they considered to be more appropriate to their newly gained qualifications:

> I'm doing full-time hours in the sports shop. I increased my hours when I graduated, but I'm still applying for other jobs.
>
> (Cameron)

With protracted transitions from part-time 'student jobs' and with a tendency to accept temporary jobs as a 'stop gap', many new graduates hold jobs that are insecure or need to 'serve time' on low grades. While those searching for graduate jobs may not be concerned about the insecurity of jobs that they are happy to regard as temporary, insecurity is a central and largely accepted part of the structure of early careers. In teaching, for example, it is not uncommon for newly qualified teachers to build up experience through taking on 'supply' work. The same is true in a number of other occupations where graduates need to get some experience to increase their chances of securing graduate careers. There is also an extent to which new graduates are drawn towards non-graduate occupations as a way of building up experience in a particular field before taking postgraduate courses. Aspiring social workers, for example, may need to work in unskilled roles in caring environments prior to being accepted on a post-graduate course in social work. Similarly, pre-course classroom experience (usually acquired by working as an unskilled classroom assistant) is often required for entry to postgraduate teaching diplomas. These practices all have an impact on the protraction and complexity of transitions from university to employment and result in a degree of insecurity and uncertainty following graduation.

> The grade I'm on, grade two, is the lowest grade. It shows you quite plainly in a wee diagram which says that you can do this and that and then go into management or become a tax inspector. It shows you the pay scales and everything, all the different training you do. I thought that it sounded brilliant. It wasn't until I started that the guy that I worked with told me that I had to stay in this job for a year before I can go and do any of them.
>
> (Flora)

Despite the 'normality' of long complex transitions involving insecurity in the early stages, there is evidence of a stratification of experiences in which females and those from less advantaged families take longer to make inroads to the labour market, are more likely to experience insecure forms of working and are less likely to obtain what could broadly be defined as graduate jobs (Smith et al. 2000; Furlong and Cartmel 2005; Adnett and Slack 2007; HESA 2007a). Indeed, those from less-advantaged families and those who attended new universities tend to make the highest number of job applications and have a lower ratio of interviews to applications (Furlong and Cartmel 2005). There is also evidence that labour market positions of graduates in their early twenties are strongly affected by educational factors such as class of degree, subject of degree and institution attended (Conlon and Chevalier 2002; Naylor et al. 2002; Purcell et al. 2005; HESA 2007b), leading to a situation where a greater proportion of graduates of the most prestigious institutions are employed in what can broadly be defined as graduate jobs (Furlong and Cartmel 2005).

At the same time, although there is a clear stratification in the early labour market experiences of graduates, we must recognize that there are clearly benefits to be derived from wider access policies. Higher education 'is a profitable path for the vast majority of potential participants' (Elias and Purcell 2004) and the clear majority of working-class graduates work in jobs that they would not have secured without having participated in higher education. As Brennan and Shah (2003) conclude, notwithstanding inequalities pertaining to admission and destination, the 'vast majority' derive considerable benefits from higher education.

Barriers

While routes between higher education and graduate careers may be complex, drawn out and even non-linear, from a social justice perspective, our concern is with the stratification of the process under which, unrelated to ability or achievement, some groups face barriers that are not encountered by others. We have already suggested that females and graduates from less-advantaged families make relatively slow progress towards graduate careers. In this section we examine some of the barriers encountered, highlighting graduates' interpretation of the difficulties they face as well as the framing of difference in policy discourse.

Despite having completed their studies, financial circumstances may represent a significant barrier to the integration of graduates into jobs commensurate with their qualifications. Less-advantaged young people may be forced to apply for all possible jobs while those who have other sources of support may be able to hold out for more desirable forms of employment. In the West of Scotland study, for example, a few respondents suggested that engagement with part-time employment stood in the way of a job-search activities focused on the graduate labour market and impeded their progress.

> If I hadn't of been working in the shop, I'd have probably managed to get something a bit quicker.
>
> (Mary)

Geographical location and the potential to become mobile to access a broader, national labour market can have an impact on patterns of entry to graduate jobs, yet having completed their studies without moving away from home, many working-class students still reside in areas with weak, local labour markets, have had no experience of independent living and may have no friends or contacts outside of their locality. In these circumstances, graduates may lack both the confidence and financial resources to establish themselves in a new locality. In the West of Scotland study, two-thirds of respondents lived in an area considered to be severely deprived (DEPCAT 5–7), and, as noted in Chapter 4, students from less-advantaged families have restricted social networks and therefore may lack an introduction to broader possibilities through peer networks. In this context, research has shown that graduates attending local universities while living at home are less likely to get a well-paid job than those who leave (Audas and Dolton 1999):

> Yeah. To begin with I kind of wanted to stay, 'cos all your friends are in Glasgow, they don't tend to move away here. But, after being away in the

summer, they [friends] were all talking, they were going to Manchester and all different places throughout the UK and you tended to find that the English people were more willing to travel and I thought, och, well, and Edinburgh's not too far.

(Louise)

In many respects, graduates from less-advantaged families are aware that they face a range of barriers not experienced by their more affluent peers. Reflecting on the ways in which they had gained from their experiences at college or university, in the West of Scotland study those from less-advantaged families tended to see themselves as having gained less from their experiences than those from more advantaged socio-economic classes and were less likely to have developed clear plans for the future. Indeed, it was clear that disadvantaged students tended to have relatively poor career management skills, not because of a lack of effort or determination, but simply because they were not sure how to go about establishing and developing graduate careers.

Respondents themselves had a keen awareness of the way in which factors relating to social background and attainments were disadvantaging them on the labour market. Qualifications (those gained at university or college as well as school-leaving qualifications) were seen as a barrier, with over a third of those in the West of Scotland study regarding their qualifications as a disadvantage in the search for work (Figure 6.1). Nearly one in five regarded the college or university they had attended as an impediment while just over one in ten thought that they were disadvantaged by the school they attended. Accent and particularly area of residence were regarded as significant while a few identified social class, gender and religion as barriers.

Having managed to negotiate the hurdles associated with entry to higher education and having successfully completed their courses, with all the difficulties that that entailed, it is clear that, however manifest, social origins

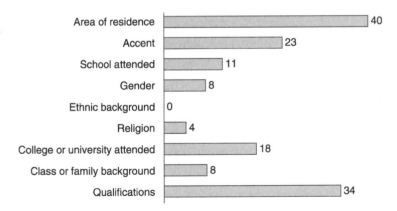

Figure 6.1 Barriers in the search for work

Source: Furlong and Cartmel (2005).

are clearly regarded as a barrier to graduate careers. While reluctant to directly identify social class as a barrier, young graduates focus on the more subtle indicators of class that are visible to employers, such as accent and area of residence. Indeed, in interviews, some expressed a feeling that the stigma associated with particular areas reduced the chances of being invited for interview or of being selected for employment:

> My accent doesn't help and employers don't go out of their way to hire people from 'Coaltoun'.
>
> (Alan)

In identifying factors that determine educational experiences and outcomes, both young people and politicians are careful to avoid the language of class, socio-economic difference, or ethnicity. Indeed, in many respects, contemporary use of the term 'employability' helps mask basic inequalities by highlighting a range of loosely related factors that impede the progress of certain groups on the labour market. Differences in employability are increasingly used to justify the stratification of experiences that cannot be reduced to objective differences such as qualifications. With graduate employers placing a high priority on soft skills, the concept of employability helps avoid the suggestion that the biases of employers have a significant impact on outcomes and individualize explanations of labour market experiences by highlighting supposed deficits in social capital.

At a basic level, the idea of employability relates to the 'capability to gain initial employment, maintain employment and obtain new employment if required' (Hillage and Pollard 1998: 1). Framed in these terms, outcomes are attributed to variations in supply rather than to patterns of demand (Brown et al. 2003; Smetherham 2006). As Brown and colleagues argue, 'the increasing policy emphasis on graduate employability, in part, reflects the increasing importance of knowledge, skills and commitments of employees as a source of efficiency, innovation and productivity, The personal is productive' (2003: 110). But in a sense it is more than that: employability is a term that wraps inequality in a discourse of legitimacy and highlights individual responsibility (Elliott and Atkinson 1998; Moreau and Leathwood 2006). In the modern economy, personal skills and qualities, which are often a euphemism for social class, are treated as resources that rival qualifications and, effectively, are recognized as a mechanism through which middle-class privileges can be maintained. While describing barriers in different ways, in many respects graduates from less-advantaged backgrounds are aware of the ways in which circumstances and resources that are linked to socio-economic difference impede their progress on the labour market.

Pecuniary and non-pecuniary rewards

Having invested heavily in higher education, graduates not only hope for interesting and rewarding employment, but have been led to expect that their degrees and diplomas will yield pecuniary advantage. While financial rewards can act as an important source of educational motivation, unrealistic wage expectations can represent a barrier to employment, yet the evidence tends to suggest that graduate wage expectation are certainly not excessively high. Among our sample of relatively disadvantaged Scots, the average salary that young people felt to be realistic for someone with their qualifications was £19,086 for males and £16,317 for females (a figure only slightly higher than the average obtained by Strathclyde University graduates in 2003). A significant gender difference in salary expectations has been noted in a range of studies: in a national survey carried out in 2005, for example, males expected starting salaries of over £2,000 more than females (£20,500 compared to £18,400) (MORI 2005). Even so, it was recognized that even 'realistic' wage expectations might not be attainable: in the West of Scotland study, the lowest salaries that respondents felt to be acceptable was some way below their expected wages (£15,202 for males and £13,885 for females). Labour market entrants recognized that any graduate premium took time to achieve and that early careers frequently involved accepting junior positions at low wages.

The significant differences in expectations regarding the graduate premium noted between males and females were also evident in relation to social classes and institutions attended. Less-advantaged young people tended to have lower wage expectations than their more-advantaged peers. In terms of lowest acceptable wages, in the West of Scotland study, those from lower working-class families were willing to accept over £1,000 less than those from other social classes (Furlong and Cartmel 2005). Those who lived in severely deprived areas had wage expectations that were over £1,000 less than those in more advantaged areas. Educational experiences also have an influence on wage expectations: in the West of Scotland study, those who attended new universities had wage expectations that were just under £4,000 less than those who attended Russell Group universities.[1]

Despite these important patterns of stratification of expectation, as Keep reminds us, 'all recent major studies show individual rates of return [to degrees] to be positive, and to be holding up well despite the expanding supply of graduates' (2004: 117). Indeed, the belief that the expansion of higher education will generate economic returns underpins the government's commitment to increasing participation and widening access and is used to legitimize funding policies. Estimates of the graduate wage premium vary, but tend to be placed in the 15–30 per cent range.

Using data from Labour Force Surveys between 1996 and 2002, McIntosh (2004) provided evidence of an increase in the graduate wage premium. Compared to those leaving education with A levels, in 2002, a graduate between the ages of 21 and 25 could expect an earnings premium of 26 per cent, while graduates between the ages of 26 and 30 could expect a premium of almost 29 per cent. This compares to an average premium of almost 16 per cent and 25 per cent, respectively, in 1996. Universities UK estimates that, over their working life, a person with an undergraduate degree will earn between 20 and 25 per cent more than someone with A levels. Represented as a lifetime earnings premium, the disparity between the two groups is in the region of £160,000 (Universities UK 2007: 2).

In 2007, the average starting salary of UK graduates was £14,515 (around 5 per cent up on 2006), although four in ten reported that their wages were lower than they had been expecting (NatWest 2007). Indeed, average starting salaries mask a wide variation in earnings that reflect the socio-economic positions of their families as well as the type of institution attended and course followed (which of course overlap considerably). Figures compiled by the *Sunday Times* (2008) show that the highest graduate starting salaries were secured by those who studied at the LSE (£27,614) and the lowest by graduates from Lampeter (£13,571).

In a UK-wide study, Brennan and Shah (2003) showed that four years after graduation men from the lower socio-economic groups earned around £1,500 less than those from the higher groups while for women the differential was about £1,000 a year. They also showed that graduates from new universities earned about £1,000 less than those from the older universities. Similar patterns of stratification have been observed in a range of studies (Christie et al. 2005; Furlong and Cartmel 2005; HESA 2007c).

Yet as a result of the low average wages received by members of lower socio-economic groups in general (and the relatively high earnings achieved by those from middle-class families who lack degrees), for men, the overall gains in average earnings associated with a degree are actually highest for low socio-economic groups (Dearden et al. 2005; Universities UK 2007). Using data from the 1970 British Birth Cohort (a nationally representative sample of those born in 1970), Dearden and colleagues showed that while male graduates from lower socio-economic groups enjoyed a wage premium of around 20 per cent, the wage premium achieved by males from high socio-economic groups was less than 14 per cent. No significant differences based on socio-economic background were found for females.

Subjects studied at university also have a significant impact on the graduate earnings premium. Figures compiled by PricewaterhouseCoopers (2007) show that, compared to a person with A levels, a graduate in medicine will earn an additional £340,315 over their lifetime, whereas the average premium is £160,061 and, at the lower end, the premium for arts subjects is just £34,494 (less than a £1,000 a year over a 40-year working life before making a reduction to account for the cost of study and accumulated interest) (Figure 6.2). There is also evidence that university entry qualifications affect lifetime earnings (PricewaterhouseCoopers 2007).

Returns to individuals from participation in higher education are not limited to those that can be identified by studying patterns of earnings. Work can provide a range of benefits which bring no obvious economic reward. In the West of Scotland survey, the vast majority of young people who were working in graduate jobs in autumn 2004 accepted their current job as they thought that the work would be interesting and challenging and thought that it would lead to an enhancement of their future career prospects.

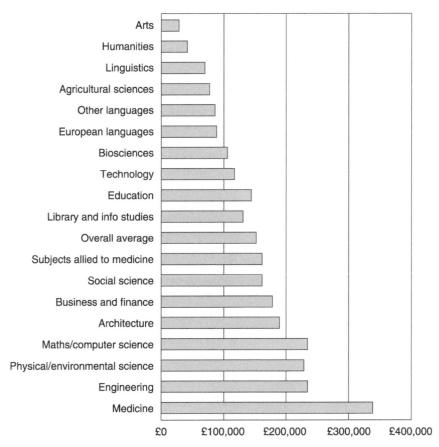

Figure 6.2 Average additional lifetime earnings of various degrees, compared to a person with two or more A levels

Source: PricewaterhouseCoopers (2007).

Opportunities for training and development were also valued, as were promotion prospects. Predictably long-term security was highlighted as important, especially by those in relatively secure graduate careers. Indeed, those who were working in graduate jobs tended to regard their jobs in a very positive light. The vast majority said that it was exactly what they wanted, that it provided opportunities for career progression and would help them broaden their experiences. Many also said that it was the best job on offer and that it allowed them to see whether this was the type of work they would like to do. Even among those who were still working in non-graduate jobs, many were able to highlight positive aspects of their jobs: a majority thought that the job would help them broaden their experiences and would allow them to see whether it was the sort of work they would like to do in the future.

At age 22, the vast majority of males (74 per cent) and females (80 per cent) expressed satisfaction with the way in which their career or education was progressing, with around three in ten (29 per cent of males and 33 per cent of females) saying that they were extremely satisfied. At the other end of the scale, just 5 per cent of males and 1 per cent of females were extremely dissatisfied. Young people from the lower working classes tended to be less satisfied than their peers from more-advantaged socio-economic backgrounds. Although nearly seven in ten young people from lower working-class families were satisfied with the progress of their careers, 31 per cent were dissatisfied. This compares to less than one in five in the more-advantaged classes (16 per cent in the professional and managerial classes and 17 per cent in the upper working classes) (Furlong and Cartmel 2005).

The extent to which young people felt satisfied with their career progress also related to their current position. Where higher education participation had led to graduate employment, or where respondents were still pursuing an educational career, the overwhelming majority felt satisfied with the progress of their careers to date. The same was true of those occupying insecure graduate jobs. However, those who occupied non-graduate jobs or marginal labour market positions were far less likely to express satisfaction: indeed, nearly four in ten (38 per cent) were dissatisfied (Furlong and Cartmel 2005).

Debt

With many changes to student funding policies and with heated political debates about the impact of student debt, young people considering higher education have a broad awareness of the fact that advanced study is likely to have consequences for personal and familial finances. However, many have a poor sense of overall cost implications, of funding sources or of likely patterns of debt accrual. A survey conducted for the NatWest Bank showed that, in 2007, sixth formers planning to go to university estimated that the cost of a three-year degree course would be close to £35,000 and expected to owe an average of £14,841 on graduation (a figure that has steadily increased from the 2000 estimate of £3,174). The investment was seen as justified in so far as almost three in four expected the experience of university to result in enhanced career prospects (NatWest 2007). As noted previously, anticipated debt appears to have a relatively small impact on the decision to enter higher education, but a much larger impact on patterns of horizontal stratification (Iannelli 2007). In other words, while debt might not deter in an absolute sense, perceived affordability is an issue that is at the heart of decisions about which courses and institutions students attend.

The average UK undergraduate student now leaves university with debts totalling £12,363 (somewhat lower than that estimated by potential entrants) with some 54 per cent leaving with debts in excess of £10,000 (NatWest 2007). The average debt incurred by male students tends to be higher than for females, mainly because men spend more at university, especially on alcohol and going out (Lea et al. 2001). There are also strong geographical differences in patterns of debt related to the fact that some cities (such as London) are far more expensive to live in than others (Durham is currently judged to be the least expensive city in which to study) (RBS 2007). However, while essential costs such as rent and transport vary significantly between cities, the availability of part-time work and average local wage rates can have a strong impact on the cost of living. Balancing living costs with income from part-time jobs, the Royal Bank of Scotland (RBS) calculated a student living index which showed Leeds to be the most cost-effective city in which to study while Nottingham was the least cost-effective: RBS suggested that the average student would be £2,238 per year better off studying in Leeds rather than Nottingham (RBS 2007).

Another factor that has a significant bearing on overall levels of debt relates to course length. Here Scottish universities which typically run four-year (rather than three) degree courses tend to involve a greater financial outlay (although the introduction of 'top-up' fees in England and the abolition of fees in Scotland has, to an extent, offset this difference). There are also some courses, such as medicine, which take longer to complete and therefore result in higher levels of debt. Less obviously, there are a range of hidden costs that lead students studying in the most prestigious institutions to incur the greatest debt. In the West of Scotland study, total debt clearly corresponded to the status hierarchy of institutions: those who had attended Russell Group institutions owed, on average, £2,608 more than those who had attended a pre-1992 university and £2,900 more than those who attended a new university. There are a variety of reasons for the differential: elite institutions may not be as inclined to develop 'work-friendly' timetabling to facilitate access to part-time jobs; accommodation costs may be greater and socializing with more affluent peers is likely to increase overall costs. In Scotland, degree students at the less prestigious universities are also more likely to leave with an ordinary rather than an honours degree which typically reduces study time by a year.

Cost differentials, together with the inability of less well-off parents to make substantial financial contributions to the education of their sons and daughters, mean that the least advantaged students are made to bear a greater share of the costs. In other words, current policies are an inversion of the principles of social justice. Evidence from several sources show that students from professional and managerial families tend to complete their courses with smaller overall debts than those from working-class families (Barke et al. 2000; Callender and Kemp 2000; Callender and Wilkinson 2003: Callender and Jackson 2005; Furlong and Cartmel 2005). In their survey of student income and expenditure, Callender and Wilkinson (2003) showed that students from the lowest social classes were most likely to take out maximum student loans while those from the highest social classes and attending the elite universities were most likely to benefit from parental generosity. Callender and Jackson (2005) showed that, on average, the poorest students left university with levels of debt that were 43 per cent higher than the richest students. In the West of Scotland study, levels of debt were greatest among those who lived in severely deprived areas and among those from single parent families.

Here it is important to recognize that all debts are not equal. Working-class students tend to owe a smaller proportion of the debt to family and friends and a much higher proportion to banks in the form of personal loans, over-drafts or credit card debt (which will incur commercial interest rates and which tend not to offer either deferred payment or low interest rates). In the West of Scotland study it was students from the poorest families who had the greatest average debts outstanding to banks whereas those from better-off families owed the most to their families (which may eventually be written off).

With students leaving higher education with variable levels of debt owed to a range of creditors, their job search patterns and their ability to move to a new area to seek work or take up an employment opportunity may be con-strained in different ways. An immediate concern of many young people who have just completed higher education is money. This is especially true where parents are unable or unwilling to offer significant support and many have significant debts to banks and to credit card companies which may need constant maintenance. Many also have immediate needs in regard to general living costs, especially if they are living apart from their parents. Concern about money can focus attention on the need for employment and when there is little sign of an early entry into a graduate job, may lead young people to seek temporary positions or may encourage them to retain the jobs held while studying. In the West of Scotland study, it was those from the least-advantaged families who were forced to take the first opportunities that came along or, more frequently, to increase the hours worked in their 'student job'. In these circumstances, some felt that they never had a proper opportunity to embark on a full-scale search for opportunities on the graduate labour market.

Conclusion

Evidence from a range of studies show clearly that, despite a sharp growth in participation in higher education, graduates continue to enjoy significant rewards in terms of employment opportunities and conditions. Overall, levels of employment are higher among graduates than among non-graduates and levels of unemployment are lower. Lifetime earnings are also higher, lending weight to the government's policy of requiring beneficiaries to contribute towards the cost of their degrees.

The types of employment available to modern graduates differ somewhat from those once thought of as typifying graduate careers. Many jobs that once recruited school or college leavers now require degrees and graduates use their skills in a wide variety of employment contexts. Moreover, graduate careers can take longer to establish and it is far from uncommon for fresh graduates to spend time working in non-graduate contexts or to be without work. Yet while these changes suggest that returns from a degree have become less predictable and have perhaps diminished in a general sense, it is important to remember that the advantages associated with higher education are still evident despite having been made available to a much larger and broader section of the population.

While we should recognize the benefits of mass higher education, it is important not to confuse wider access with social justice. Higher education is highly stratified and some groups of participants, especially those from less-advantaged families, clearly derive far fewer benefits than those from more affluent families. The lines of stratification are complex; prior qualifications make a difference, as do subjects studied and types of institution attended. In this context, Archer argues that the stratification of employment outcomes is an inevitable consequence of institutional stratification:

> [T]he two-tier system of higher education prevents real social mobility across class boundaries for working-class students. As long as working-class students remain disadvantaged through their concentration within less prestigious institutions, then they will remain disadvantaged in an overcrowded job market.
>
> (2003: 134)

As Brennan and Naidoo argue,

> Where once entry to higher education was the passport to power and privilege, today it may only be entry to a relatively small number of institutions that can provide equivalent opportunities. But this should not hide the fact that entry to *any* form of higher education is likely to maintain or improve a person's life chances and this is especially the case for people from disadvantaged social groups.
>
> (2007: 29)

While it is true that powerful differences are associated with traditional and new universities, even when these factors are controlled for, graduates from disadvantaged backgrounds still fare less well in terms of employment-related outcomes (Brennan and Shah 2003).

If we are to accept the principle that beneficiaries should contribute towards the cost of their education, we also need to recognize that a socially just approach would ensure that contributions were broadly commensurate with gains. In reality, under the current UK systems, the opposite is true. Those who can least afford to pay and those who gain the least from higher education end up paying more, in absolute and relative terms, for their education. As we have seen, the wage differentials typical of those in the highest paid subject groups are ten times higher than the lowest and, across the board, females and working-class students earn significantly less than their more-advantaged peers.

7
Building a socially just system of higher education

> As institutions charged with education, research and training, our
> purpose is not to be construed as that of handmaidens of industry,
> implementers of the skills agenda, or indeed engines for promoting
> social justice . . . [P]romoting social mobility is not our core mission.
> (Alison Richard, Vice-Chancellor, Cambridge University,
> quoted in *The Times* 2008)

Introduction

Throughout this book we have discussed the various ways in which the laud-
able aim of providing a system of higher education built on the principles
of social justice has been thwarted by government policy and by the action
(and inaction) of universities. Despite the introduction of a wide range of
reforms and the establishment of a mass system of higher education, those
occupying privileged positions have always found ways, usually without much
effort, to ensure that their offspring monopolize places in the elite universities and enter the most prestigious courses. Through their ability to
navigate and manipulate educational structures, from primary to tertiary
levels, the middle classes have helped ensure that levels of downward mobility remain low while meritocratic opportunities for upward mobility among
the working classes are blocked or severely restricted. While it is all too
easy to identify specific British policies and practices that facilitate these
processes, we must recognize that in all advanced societies, including those
that take social justice much more seriously than is the case in the UK, the
privileged classes are able to use education to protect their offspring while
the working classes make relatively few inroads. Mechanisms may differ, but
outcomes across advanced societies are remarkably similar. While it is hard to
disagree with Rikowski's (2000) claim that social justice and capitalism are
fundamentally incompatible, there is still immense value in identifying ways
in which opportunities for working-class students can be enhanced.

In this chapter, our aim is to discuss some of the preconditions for building a socially just system of higher education. Our aim is to 'think the unthinkable' and explore not only the 'safe' options, but also the sorts of changes that (sometimes irrationally and at other times linked to self-interest) might be rejected out of hand by key stakeholders such as university administrators, academics, politicians and middle-class parents. First of all, we need to set some parameters. In the context of a book on higher education, we do not intend to redesign nursery, primary or secondary education; although radical reforms are overdue (which range from the universal provision of nursery education to the abolition of private and selective secondary schools) and do have a powerful impact on social justice. Indeed, without radical reform of primary and secondary provision, the social justice agenda at the tertiary level is seriously undermined. Confining discussion to the higher educational sector, we have to begin with the recognition that potential applicants are a hugely unequal group: they range from wealthy applicants whose families have had a long tradition of attending university to the offspring of unemployed and marginalized parents who have had no contact with higher education and have little awareness of its structures, procedures or benefits: they also range from the high-flying applicant with straight As at A level, to the young person or mature entrant who has under-developed academic abilities and who lacks the usual entry qualifications. While the prerogative of universities to discriminate on the basis of school attainments (which continue to be regarded as a proxy for ability rather than for social class) has been thought of as their inalienable right, school-level qualifications must be recognized as a key mechanism through which social justice is blocked.

In the opening chapter we briefly explored some contrasting views of the purpose of the modern university and the ways in which these developed over the past century. In this concluding chapter we attempt to rethink the priorities of a system of higher education that has social justice embedded in its mission statement, not simply as a platitude, but as a core aim that is recognized by all members of the university community. We begin then, by trying to clarify the role of a modern university system suited to serve a diverse population in an age of mass participation. Having established some parameters, we examine some key components of the university system, from selection and access to funding and the curriculum; in each of these contexts the aim is to reflect on the sorts of changes required by a system driven by a commitment to social justice.

Putting social justice at the centre of higher educational policy

In the light of evidence presented in the preceding chapters, from the standpoint of social justice, it would be fair to argue that British universities are not fit for purpose. Yet many vice-chancellors, such as Cambridge's

Alison Richard, would argue that the role of the university is not to promote or facilitate a social justice agenda. Others, particularly those in charge of some of the new universities, would vehemently disagree with her proposition. Given that higher education is central to processes of social reproduction in modern societies, it is somewhat strange that vice-chancellors are able to distance themselves from a process that is unfolding within their own estates. Other stakeholders are clear that the facilitation of social mobility is one of the core purposes of higher education: young people and their parents see university as paving the way to rewarding careers while politicians are all too aware that university access policies may block opportunities for the working classes.

The lack of clarity among vice-chancellors (especially those in charge of Russell Group universities) about something that should be a core part of their mission statement requires some clarification. Two possible explanations spring to mind. First, that the senior management in the old universities genuinely fail to understand that prior attainment and qualifications cannot be regarded as a satisfactory proxy for merit or potential. In other words, they fail to grasp the idea that qualifications may be little more than a proxy for class and privilege and wrongly assume that giving preference to hot-housed middle-class applicants who are largely able to jump academic hurdles, helps protect academic standards. Second, with a lack of clarity about the core role of a modern university, institutions may downplay roles that they are not performing well by arguing that such activities are not actually part of their remit (viz. Alison Richard of Cambridge, and Anthony Smith, president of Magdalen College, Oxford, who argued that higher education must not become a 'branch of social welfare' (*Guardian* 2004b)). If a university is not performing well in terms of widening access, then senior managers might well argue that their strengths and priorities lie elsewhere. In a similar manner, a lecturer who cannot teach effectively may argue that research is their primary role.

Unsurprisingly, a browse through university mission statements shows that new universities frequently emphasize their role in promoting social justice, whereas older universities prefer to highlight research and teaching excellence. By way of example, the opening sentence of Central Lancashire Universities' mission statement is 'we value and practise equality of opportunity', while Wolverhampton University states that it 'is committed to being an agent for social inclusion and social change'. In contrast, Edinburgh University sees its main role as the 'advancement and dissemination of knowledge and understanding', and promises to 'sustain and develop its position as a research and teaching institution of the highest international quality'. While Edinburgh University expects to 'contribute to society', it makes no mention of social justice, social inclusion or equality of opportunity (and obviously there are many ways that universities can contribute to society that have no impact whatsoever on the social justice agenda).

To an extent, the different priorities embedded in university mission statements reflect both a diversity of traditions, cultures and priorities as well as confusion about what universities are for. We can probably formulate a statement that encapsulates the priorities of all primary or secondary schools, but it would be difficult to find agreement on the priorities of universities in a general sense. Indeed, Greenwood suggests that universities combine 'a mixed, confusing and even contradictory set of activities' (2007: 98) which can be linked to their diverse origins and histories, while Bourgeois and colleagues refer to their 'multiple and ambiguous roles and missions (1999: 41). Reflecting their origins as elite institutions, the older universities like to think of themselves as 'research intensive', as providing stimulating and well-resourced homes for world-class research 'stars' and as making substantial contributions to the UK economy and to knowledge globally. While traditional universities might acknowledge the need to adjust to modern contexts, they are reluctant to abandon their claim to elite status. Linked to their core research and scholarly activities, an important but somewhat secondary activity involves passing on their knowledge to the next generation of academics through accepting a limited number of 'bright' students judged to be capable of absorbing their wisdom. Of course, research is not always well funded so admitting students has important financial benefits: the danger of course is that the student experience may be of little interest to academics who may regard them as little more than 'cash cows'. New universities, which were established to serve a broader, more localized, population frequently recognize that their main strengths lie in teaching and realize that research funds are never going to tip the balance sheet. With their roots in the vocational training sector, teaching the masses has always been their *raison d'être*, and teaching loads have tended to be much higher than in the established sector. Even so, some staff do have ambitions to establish research-centred careers and may not prioritize teaching.

To what extent should we tolerate diversity in a system responsible for providing tertiary education for the masses in a context where equal opportunities are prioritized? If, as Gallacher and colleagues (1996) suggest, university policies are central to social change and if one of their key roles is to help shape 'a democratic and civilized society' (Välimaa and Hoffman 2007), can we accept a polarized system in which some institutions are unashamedly elitist while others welcome students who lack the usual entry requirements? We suggest that the current pattern of diversity at the undergraduate level will inevitably provide a context in which the established middle classes are able to perpetuate their privileges while the working classes are largely excluded from the main avenues of advancement. As we suggested earlier, the current tertiary system bears many similarities to the selective system of secondary education that existed prior to comprehensivization: a system that was regarded as anachronistic in an age where equal opportunities were being prioritized. In these circumstances, a polarized system of higher education should not be tolerated by those who value social justice.

Smith and Webster have argued that universities today are 'narrowly instrumental' and 'passive' and have constantly failed to address their purpose in the modern world (1997: 4). If this is true, and we believe it is, then to move forward and establish a modern system of higher education, which is suitable for the education of a majority of the population and designed to ensure equal opportunities and facilitate social mobility, requires radical solutions. One solution would be to concentrate *all* undergraduate teaching in those institutions willing to commit wholeheartedly to the principles of social justice and to explicitly recognize that one of their core missions is to promote social mobility. It may be that some universities would find such a move unpalatable and would be willing to sacrifice income from undergraduate teaching in order to continue to prioritize 'pure' knowledge and remain relatively free of 'fashion and social need' or other powerful 'unacademic forces' (Minogue 1973: 60). As long as these elitist institutions were prevented from introducing private undergraduate provision in competition with the state sector, there are no strong reasons why some universities should not focus entirely on research and postgraduate teaching. Indeed, where an elitist culture permeates institutional life, there is good reason to judge their environments to be unsuitable for modern undergraduate teaching in a society that values social justice.

To put social justice at the centre of higher education policy, institutions that offer an undergraduate curriculum must, first and foremost, create an environment which promotes social mobility and provide opportunities for cross-class socialization. While academics tend to identify closely with their discipline and place a premium on disciplinary learning, students may take a much more instrumental approach. They may regard subject-based knowledge as a vehicle for developing a broad range of (hard and soft) skills which will ultimately help secure future job opportunities in fields totally unrelated to their field of study. Similarly, many employers may have little interest in the subjects studied by job applicants, although they may expect students to demonstrate motivation and a successful engagement with advanced learning. A university fit for the twenty-first century must be designed to meet the needs of *all* stakeholders without unjustifiably privileging the academic viewpoint.

Although radical change is necessary in order to build a mass university system capable of contributing to a more socially just society, at the level of government policy, debates about social justice and higher education tend to be framed relatively narrowly. By and large, discussion tends to prioritize two areas, access to higher education and financial arrangements for students, with recent attention also focused on non-completion and, linked to a desire to increase survival rates, consideration of ways of enhancing the student experience. And in each of these areas, the debate has been framed very narrowly. There has been little appetite to question the link between qualifications and admissions policy or to contemplate financial support systems that facilitate geographical mobility or financial independence from parental support. Recent policies have also tended to reinforce the idea that higher education should be completed in advance of full-time labour market engagement and that the experience should essentially be a linear one. In reality, a much more holistic approach is necessary: one which focuses on the needs and aspirations of a diverse student group in an era where linear progression has become less common and where higher education may be just one activity in a broad portfolio. Whereas the shift from an elite to a mass system of higher education should have led to a rethink in the role of the university and the nature of the student experience, in reality, universities have tended to provide 'more of the same', albeit with some concessions to students frequently labelled as 'non-traditional': a group who might be thought of more positively as the vanguard of the modern order.

Access to higher education

The question of who should be allowed access to higher education remains highly controversial, with McNay going as far as to argue that 'the barriers erected by some institutions have been more seditious than the barricades of 1960s students' (2006: 225). There are two issues to consider here. First, what proportion of the population are capable of benefitting from higher education and deserve support from the public purse? Second, on what criteria should we decide who gets access to the most prestigious institutions and courses?

There can be no scientific answer to the question about the proportion of a cohort who should experience higher education. A couple of decades ago the idea that one in two should experience higher education would have been laughable (as would the idea that all young people should remain in education until 18) and while today the view that 50 per cent are capable of benefitting from higher education has not found universal acceptance, in some countries rates of participation are far higher. Globalization and labour market change are key drivers of changing demand, but there is also recognition that skill development in itself stimulates demand and can affect firms' investment decisions. While important, economic factors are not the only justification for investment in higher education. An educated population may display greater levels of civic engagement and can impact on processes of social reproduction through their role in educating the next generation. Education may also be undertaken for personal fulfilment, without instrumental justification.

For the middle classes, questions about access are underpinned by the recognition that some institutions and some courses are likely to bring about greater economic gains in the long run and are more likely to protect against downward social mobility. Hence investment in private primary and secondary education may be justified in terms of access to elite institutions. Yet the secondary qualifications gained by their offspring tend to be regarded as 'objective' indicators of achievement and merit, rather than as commodities that have been purchased within an educational market place. Consequently any move by the universities to devalue 'purchased' qualifications by challenging their objectivity (by accepting lower entrance qualifications from state-educated applicants, for example) lead to claims that universities are engaged in a process of 'social engineering', are helping erode academic standards and are failing to recognize the efforts and achievements of 'bright' middle-class applicants.

The use of national qualifications such as A levels, Highers or HNC/ HNDs to aid the selection process by identifying the most able candidates is problematic because of the very different conditions under which these forms of education take place. Some are taught in small classes with world-class facilities while others have to endure overcrowded classrooms which they may share with disruptive fellow pupils who occupy much of the time of the class teacher. Under these conditions, it is only fair that admissions officers employ a system of weighting in an attempt to take account of the privileges and disadvantages of candidates.

While discussion about fair access frequently focuses on entrance qualifications, an alternative approach could involve a system of open access under which anyone who wished to study at tertiary level would automatically be granted access, irrespective of prior attainments. Some European universities utilize an open access system fairly successfully, although the downside is that it is associated with relatively high dropout rates at the end of the first year. Yet as Rawls (1971) argued, a socially just system can only be built if all forms of selection are removed. It is true that an open access system would require fairly radical changes in the university curriculum: a proper 'beginner's introduction' to all subjects would be required as some students would lack an adequate background knowledge of specific disciplines. Obviously within a system of higher education specialization must take place and there has to be the facility for learning of the highest order. In a mass system, though, specialization must take place at a later stage, such as at the Masters level, otherwise it will inevitably result in stratification and the reproduction of advantage.

With an increase in the number of students living with their parents for financial reasons, for many, choices are effectively framed by local provision. Those who can afford to move have access to a national market, while poorer students may be forced to accept whatever provision is available locally. To create a fairer system of access it is necessary either to put a system of financial support in place that makes mobility for all feasible, or to move to a system of local provision for all. To an extent, the government's approach has been to support a catchment-based approach for poorer students while leaving a market-based model intact for the middle classes. Bill Rammell, the former universities minister, for example, argued that 'we need now to address widening participation by strengthening the structural links between schools, colleges and universities. For universities, direct engagement with secondary education is the natural next step in widening participation' (*Guardian* 2008b: 8).[1] As part of their wider access strategies, many universities have established links with local schools serving high deprivation catchments. Such links may aim to stimulate knowledge about provision and enhance educational aspirations and sometimes involve commitments to accept those who meet agreed performance thresholds.

Another approach to widening access involves the recognition of non-standard qualifications, ranging from a university's own access courses to accredited work-based training. In this context, firms such as McDonald's are now offering diplomas for employees who undertake a programme of structured training: diplomas that may facilitate entry to higher education.[2] While some of these industry-based programmes have been sneered at by the middle classes, they could make a valuable contribution to the wider access agenda by offering a valuable alternative to traditional approaches to wider access which encourages re-engagement among early school leavers.

Funding

In Chapter 3 we described some of the funding regimes implemented in different countries and examined their implications for social justice. We want to return to this issue again here, briefly, to highlight what we regard as the central principles underlying a system that prioritizes equal opportunities. There are three core principles: first, no one should be in a position where they are excluded from higher education for financial reasons; second, any system of funding should be free at the point of use and any repayments structured in such a way that no one should be deterred by a fear of debt; and third, the funding of students and institutions should not lead to a situation where undergraduates at some universities enjoy superior learning conditions or levels of support than at others.

Clearly under the current funding arrangements in the UK as a whole, people are passing up on opportunities to attend higher education due to a lack of funding and also making choices on the basis of cost. As we have seen, well-qualified students from poorer families opt for local institutions as the costs of mobility are too high and choose shorter courses to keep costs down. Thus the funding regimes that are in place effectively help block long-range social mobility and reproduce class-based advantage. With many young people unable to count on financial support from their families, a socially just system of funding must be structured in such a way that all students are provided directly with funds that would allow them access to a full range of educational options. If parental contributions form part of a funding package, the contribution should perhaps be collected by government and transferred to the student's bank account to ensure that parents meet their obligations: currently many do not.

Although student loans are part of the funding regime in many countries, it is important to ensure that students from poorer families are not deterred by concern over long-term affordability. In some ways, these concerns are linked to a lack of familiarity with higher education, with a lack of confidence in the economic benefits of higher education and by the sheer size of the likely debt in relation to family income and wealth. Here a post-study contribution to a pooled debt, structured in terms of income and collected via the general taxation system, has strong benefits from a social justice perspective.

In the UK, the stratification of higher education is not simply about status differentials, it also relates to the funding of institutions and even to the levels of support provided to students from less-advantaged families. Quite simply, elite institutions are able to offer their students superior learning conditions and provide poorer students with larger bursaries. In contrast, in Scandinavia, despite differences in prestige between institutions, all are treated equally by funding policies (Barr 2001). In the UK, on account of differential funding, students at the older universities tend to have more favourable staff–student ratios. In the City of Liverpool, for example, at John Moores University (a new university) staff–student ratios are nearly three times higher than at Liverpool University (a Russell Group institution) (*Times Higher* 2008c). Nationally the number of students per academic ranges from 3.6 at the London School of Hygiene and Tropical Medicine to 26.4 at Middlesex University (*Times Higher Education Supplement* 2007c).

Changes in systems of funding have also led to a situation where, in England, less advantaged students in older (and wealthier) institutions can expect higher levels of financial support than those in newer institutions. As a condition for being allowed to set student fees at the highest permitted level (currently £3,225 per annum which is charged by virtually all English universities), institutions have to top slice £310 per student to fund bursaries for those from less advantaged families. With relatively few poorer students in older universities, this effectively means that they are able to make larger payments to those who are eligible. A bursary recipient in a Russell Group university currently (2006/07) receives an average of £1,764 compared to an eligible student at a new university who receives an average of £716 (*Times Higher* 2008b). A suggestion by the Higher Education Policy Institute (Chester and Bekhradnia 2008) that a national system of bursaries (funded by top-slicing institutions directly) would lead to a fairer system has been rejected out of hand by the Russell Group while welcomed by post-1992 institutions and the National Union of Students (*Times Higher* 2008b).

Curriculum

Discussion about the place of the curriculum in a system of higher education designed to promote social mobility has so far been limited, and the universities have shown few signs of a willingness to engage in a radical re-structuring of provision. Indeed, the universities have largely been able to get away with an inflexible approach in which they regard themselves as guardians of standards and as the only legitimate adjudicators of curriculum content. In an era where relatively few participated in higher education, such a system may have been acceptable, but mass participation under conditions of social justice requires a radical rethink of the nature of provision. The higher educational curriculum should not simply be about educating within narrow disciplinary boundaries, it must be designed to engage and stimulate a diverse range of students and prepare them for life beyond the university.[3] Universities should be prepared to introduce students to subjects they have not previously studied and ensure that they prevent early specialization. Moreover, universities have a duty to make efforts to ensure that subject areas do not become dominated by students from particular social classes and should facilitate cross-class socialization.

It is clear that few UK universities adopt these principles and most students are educated within relatively narrow curricula boundaries. Although the changes required are radical, Melbourne University, one of the top institutions in Australia, has recently introduced changes that incorporate many of these ideas. Under the 'Melbourne Model' which was introduced in 2008, 96 undergraduate courses have been replaced by six broad undergraduate programmes[4] which provide a foundation for graduate professional degrees, higher research degrees or a career. To encourage breadth of study, a quarter of courses studied must be selected from a programme other than which the student is enrolled. The objective of the reform was to 'produce graduates who are suited to the challenges of changing workplaces in the twenty-first century and equip them with a range of abilities to enable them to engage with local and global communities' (www.provost.unimelb.edu.au/about_us/melbourne_model, accessed 25 September 2008). Such an approach allows students to defer specialization by delaying choices that may overly restrict future options and ensures that professionally orientated courses such as law, medicine and education become graduate entry courses. Early evidence suggests that many potential students view the changes favourably, although there have been predicable objections by academics who regard the model as promoting mediocrity (www.wikipedia.org/wiki/melbourne_model). Other Australian universities appear to be following Melbourne's lead: the University of Western Australia and Macquarie University have both recently announced plans to drastically reduce the number of undergraduate courses (*Times Higher* 2008d). Perhaps it is time for the UK to follow suit. Indeed, Barr (2008) has recently argued for a return to a broad-based curriculum so as to promote the establishment of an educated and critical public.

Aside from curriculum content, modes of delivery also have implications for social justice. With many students combining employment with study, institutions should not assume that work engagement is flexible and that students can prioritize (frequently inflexible) lecture and seminar attendance. Employers may put pressure on student workers to work extra shifts and efficient time management may result in students deciding against travel to university on days when they have a very small number of scheduled contact hours. Although socializing with peers is a central part of the student experience, with modern communications there is no reason why web-based back-ups[5] should not be available to those unable to attend specific sessions and, in the case of lab-based teaching, flexible scheduling should be considered essential. The tradition of universities being 'hungry institutions' has to change in the interests of social justice.

There is evidence suggesting that students are not overly enthusiastic about traditional lecture- and seminar-based approaches to learning and prefer active, student-centred modes of delivery (Harvey and Drew 2006). Harvey and Drew suggest that such approaches provide learners with the types of transferable skill required in their future working lives and assist their development as autonomous learners. In Denmark, Roskilde University makes extensive use of problem-orientated approaches rather than traditional teaching methods. Students undertake a range of group work projects in place of lecture-based courses and, drawing on various resources, take greater responsibility for their own learning than is the case in more traditional universities. Such an approach is both popular with students and is pedagogically sound.

There is also an urgent need to rethink the assumptions of the linearity of educational careers than underpin higher educational policy. Not only do students combine education and employment in a variety of ways, they also need to be able to take time out or change their level of involvement from time to time. As Wyn (2009) has noted, student learning is not confined to that which occurs in formal educational settings, and students may develop complementary and valued skills through employment and through their leisure pursuits. In this respect it can be argued that the structure of higher education is not suited to the age of late modernity. As we have argued, it is important to structure delivery in ways which enable students to combine work and study more effectively, but changes have to go beyond more flexible timetabling. At the present time, the government imposes financial penalties on those institutions that have poor rates of retention and, perhaps more significantly, publishes league tables of retention rates so as to publicly embarrass institutions that have high 'dropout' rates. Effectively, the policy penalizes those institutions that take wider access seriously by recruiting large numbers of non-traditional students. But the implications of such policies are far-reaching. First, it encourages institutions to increase their surveillance of students in an attempt to identify potential 'dropouts' (and in the process places pressure on students who may be juggling work and study to 'normalize' their attendance). As a result, we are seeing the introduction of intrusive forms of monitoring, such as one recently introduced at Glamorgan University which involves the use of electronic monitoring devices triggered by computer chips embedded in students' key rings (Baty 2006). The system, appropriately known as 'uni-nanny', is likely to be used by other institutions in the near future (Baker and Brown 2007).

Second, rather than facilitating flexible higher educational careers which may involve repeated breaks in study and variable levels of participation (from full-time to a single module) in a career that could span more than a decade, institutions still tend to think in terms of a three- or four-year undergraduate career and regard more extended forms of participation as problematic. A full-time three- or four-year degree should no longer be considered the gold standard.[6]

Third, as young adults become the drivers of their own biographies, navigating increasing complex pathways, negotiating and identifying forms of learning that assist in career development and life-fulfilment, the pressure to make them full participants in the design of the higher educational experience becomes ever more powerful. Students may not have the disciplinary knowledge necessary to determine the finer detail of curriculum content, but there is a legitimate expectation that they be involved in discussions about the shape of the curriculum, the mode of delivery and the nature of the learning experience. To facilitate full participation and to ensure that under-represented groups maximize the potential benefits of higher education, there is also clearly a need to provide quality support services, including effective advisers. While many institutions have some form of advisory service, few explicitly target students from less-advantaged families.[7]

Conclusion

In modern societies, universities must be prepared to play a leading role in the creation of a socially just society. They cannot achieve this alone, but they must recognize that they are important and influential players in the process. Radical changes are necessary, many of which can be achieved without the need for significant additional funds, but little progress will be made while universities adopt a timid approach and remain reluctant to upset their traditional middle-class stakeholders. As Brennan and Naidoo argue, 'for disadvantaged groups to change places with advantaged groups requires some downward mobility to make space for some upward mobility' (2007: 32) and there is a need to direct policy towards finding effective ways of restricting middle-class advantage. Here Archer and colleagues are clear that 'large scale change remains unlikely while government funding protects and perpetuates elitism' (2003: 197).

To an extent, universities' increasing tendency to develop marketing strategies and to prioritize income generation has had a detrimental impact on their commitment to widening access and there is often a conflict between universities' business strategies and their role in civil society. As Hill suggests, 'Education as a social institution has been subordinated to international market goals including the language and self-conceptualisation of education themselves . . . Within Universities . . . the language of education has been very widely replaced by the language of the market' (2003: 7). Indeed, as we argued earlier, marketing strategies are used by universities in ways that help perpetuate social divisions. The impact of marketization goes beyond language. It can encourage university managers to target more lucrative fee-paying students from overseas, leading to increased competition for places among local students which may help displace 'non-traditional' applicants. Ehrenberg (2007) also highlights the extent to which various league tables relating to status and performance impact on university strategies. With US institutions frequently engaged in an 'arms race' (Ehrenberg 2007: 190) to attain prestigious league table positions, he argues that universities are effectively encouraged to prioritize factors that have the strongest bearing on position (such as qualifications) and led to downplay factors that contribute little to their status (such as the number of students from low-income families).

A starting point for any significant change has to involve debate about the purpose of higher education. A university system that places an emphasis on the generation of knowledge for the sake of knowledge and remains unconcerned about practical benefit or the social and economic contribution of university education is unlikely to appeal to large numbers of students from less-advantaged families (Wakeling 2005). At the same time, the contribution of the university system has to go beyond the function of 'sorting, weeding and cooling' in a dispassionate manner (Côté and Allahar 2007: 41).

A university which is effective in terms of its role in the promotion of social justice needs to ensure that measures permeate the whole breadth of university activity: from access through to the curriculum and to careers guidance. Commenting on equity in higher education, Skilbeck argues for the need to 'integrate policy relating to under-represented groups into all aspects of the institution [and] ensure their views are represented in planning and decision making' (2000: n.p). In these terms, a full commitment to social justice might also involve the development of policies towards staff recruitment which result in a greater diversity of personnel (McNay 2006): such an approach may secure greater involvement and enhance the motivation of under-represented groups of students who at present are largely taught by white middle-class lecturers in institutions headed by white middle-class males.

Appendix: The West of Scotland study

In this book we have drawn on interviews conducted as part of three related projects, funded by the Joseph Rowntree Foundation, between 1999 and 2004 (Forsyth and Furlong 2000, 2003; Furlong and Cartmel 2005). The projects followed a cohort drawn from four areas in the West of Scotland who were first contacted in their final year of school and re-contacted throughout their time at university or college and (for those who followed relatively linear pathways) in the initial stages of their graduate careers. The study employed quantitative and qualitative methods, although with the quantitative data described at length in the three published reports here we primarily focus on the qualitative interviews carried out at several different time points during the course of the five-year project.

An initial sample of 516 young people was selected during the final part of the last year of schooling (S6) from a total of 16 schools which were either located in disadvantaged areas or located in remote areas where young people would have to leave home in order to enter higher (and in some cases further) education. The schools were drawn from four areas (Glasgow City, North Lanarkshire, Ayrshire and Argyll) and, in general terms, the sample could be described as 'qualified but disadvantaged'. All schools had below the Scottish national average level of school-leavers entering higher education, yet had a sufficient number of pupils studying in sixth year for a viable sample of qualified young people to be recruited.

The initial self-complete questionnaires were completed in the classroom under the supervision of a researcher, with further questionnaires despatched by post. Response rates for each subsequent survey sweep were very good, ranging between 72 per cent and 81 per cent. By the time the three stages of the project were finished, those who had completed each questionnaire had responded six times over the course of five years (Table A.1).

Without providing detail of the sample demographics at each stage of the survey (full details are provided in the individual reports), almost three-quarters of the initial sample lived in severely deprived areas (DEPCATs 5–7 on the Carstairs-Morris scale[1]) whereas none lived in the most affluent

Table A.1 Summary of responses to the three projects

Date	Average age	Typical educational stage	Number of interviews conducted	Number of questionnaires despatched	Response rate (%)
Spring 1999	17	School sixth year	–	516	100
Autumn 1999	17.6	HE 1st year	–	515	77
Spring 2000	17.6	HE 1st year	44	–	–
Autumn 2000	18.6	HE 2nd year	–	395	81
Spring 2001	19.0	HE 2nd year	40	–	–
Autumn 2001	19.6	HE 3rd year	–	395	78
Spring 2002	20.0	HE 3rd year	41	–	–
Autumn 2003	21.6	HE 4th year	–	394	72
Spring 2004	22.0		40	–	–
Autumn 2004	22.6		–	332	76

areas (DEPCAT 1). Just under a third of the sample were from single parent families while more than one in eight had at least one unemployed parent. Almost one third of the sample received a bursary to assist them to stay on at school which can also be taken as an indicator of socio-economic disadvantage. The sample was skewed towards females from the outset, with 57 per cent of the original sample being women, which reflects patterns of educational participation in these areas rather than sample bias. Only 14 respondents were from ethnic minority backgrounds: a figure broadly in line with ethnic representation in the population at that time.

During the course of the three projects, four rounds of face-to-face interviews were conducted, involving a total of 165 individual interviews with some people being interviewed on more than one occasion (Table A.1). The criteria for selection varied at each interview round. In the first round, we focused on two groups; those who had progressed to higher education and who were eligible for full or partial (of at least 50 per cent) fee waivers and those who had not progressed to higher education and who received a means-tested bursary while at school or lived in a deprived or remote area. The 81 interviewees conducted as part of the second project were selected so as to cover as wide a variety of educational pathways as possible (using information collected through the postal surveys). The 40 interviewees selected in the third project were selected from among those who had left higher education and entered the labour market (employed or unemployed), with these interviews focusing on post university experiences and plans for the future.

Notes

1 Higher education and social justice

1 Across the UK there are some significant differences in policies towards higher education and differences, especially relating to funding, are becoming more pronounced. In this book we highlight such differences where they are relevant, but refer to the UK where differences between England, Scotland, Wales and Northern Ireland are of little consequence.
2 In Scotland, around 50 per cent of young people currently enter higher education, broadly defined.
3 Foreword to the Dearing Report (1997).
4 The jurisdiction of the Office of Fair Access is limited to England.

2 Unequal access

1 Financial penalties are relatively small and unlikely to concern major research-led universities.
2 Classes 1, 2 and 3.
3 Initially the figure was £3,000 but inflationary allowances have raised the 2009 figure to £3,225.
4 The target applies to England and Wales. Scotland has already achieved 50 per cent participation.
5 Admissions interviews are most common in elite institutions and for high status courses such as medicine.
6 Gallacher and Osborne (2005a) argue that, given the nature of the HNC/HND curricula, such reservations are partly justified.

3 Reinforcing inequality through funding policies

1 The 2004 Higher Education Bill did not apply to Scotland or Wales.

2 Federally funded 'Pell Grants' are available to students whose families have incomes below $40,000 and provide a maximum of $4,310 to low income students (*Washington Post* 2007). In 2002, nationally nearly three in ten undergraduates at four-year institutions received Pell Grants, compared to less than one in five in the most selective public universities (Heller 2004; Ehrenberg 2007).

3 Estimates of rates of high school completion range from 66 to 88 per cent (Heckman and LaFontaine 2007; Stone 2009). Around 64 per cent enter higher education (OECD 2004) with around 42 per cent of high school graduates completing a degree course within ten years of enrolling (Rosenbaum 2002).

4 There are a range of barriers that make it difficult for students to transfer from community colleges to four-year institutions, including finance, geographical obstacles and academic issues. There is evidence showing that those from lower socioeconomic backgrounds and members of ethnic minorities find it most difficult to make a successful transfer (Bonham 2005).

5 Despite their great wealth, the annual spend of Ivy League universities on student support represents a very small proportion of their endowment yield. In 2006, despite yields in excess of 15 per cent, both Harvard and Yale spent just 0.3 per cent of their endowments on student aid (*Journal of Blacks in Higher Education* 2008).

6 There is evidence suggesting that, over the past two decades, only ten of the highest ranked US universities have seen an increase in the proportion of undergraduates from low income families (*Journal of Blacks in Higher Education* 2008).

7 In 2004, average student debt was $34,150 (Usher 2005).

8 In the Netherlands loan agreements are even more generous with debt being written off after 15 years and repayments suspended during periods when the graduate has a low income (Usher 2005).

9 One such approach is to enrol for short-cycle courses of higher education such as HNC or HND that provide opportunities to transfer into the later years of a degree programme. Like the US community college system, some may face barriers to further study and short-cycle programmes tend to route students towards less prestigious institutions (Gallacher and Osborne 2005b).

10 The Scottish public and government still largely reject the idea of tuition fees and there is significant support for the reintroduction of grants.

11 Here one might like to note that the government department responsible for higher education in England and Wales spent £5.7 billion on student loans and grants in 2008, while the Ministry of Defence spent a total of £35.6 billion including almost £3 billion on operational spending in Iraq and Afghanistan (excluding normal staff and operating costs of the Army, Navy and Air Force) (*Guardian* 2008a).

12 Respondents were progressing to higher education at a time when Scottish students were expected to contribute to fees unless their family income was particularly low.

13 In 2006, the NatWest Bank showed that the average undergraduate was expected to accumulate a debt of £13,252 with 57 per cent expressing concern about their debt.

14 While the SNP manifesto promised to reintroduce grants, no action has yet been taken.

4 Fragmented contexts

1 UCAS points are calculated from the various qualifications that potential students set out on their university application forms.

5 Changing pathways, altered experiences

1 In the 1950s many non-completers left to take up job offers and, among those who failed to gain degrees, failing final exams was much more common, accounting for around one in five non-completers (Committee on Higher Education 1963).

6 Differential rewards

1 Some of this difference relates to the concentration of disadvantaged students in the less prestigious institutions.

7 Building a socially just system of higher education

1 Of course such initiatives have a relatively long history with some even targeting primary schools.
2 There have been examples of similar work-based initiatives, both in the UK and in other countries, but they have often failed due to a lack of ongoing commitment by employers and through poor system flexibility (Osborne and Young 2006).
3 In this context, Barr (2008) argues for the return of a broad-based curriculum centred on the establishment of an educated and critical public and criticizes narrow curricula approaches and fragmentation of disciplines.
4 Arts, biomedicine, commerce, environment, music and science.
5 McNay found that nearly eight in ten university staff interviewed thought that in the near future 'at least 25 per cent of their courses [will be delivered] through packaged/independent learning' (2006: 221). However, we recognize that to be effective web-based materials need to be well designed from a pedagogical perspective.
6 Gallacher and Osborne (2005b) rightly highlight the advantages of promoting short-cycle programmes of higher education (such as HNC/HND) followed by part-time provision to degree level so as to enable participants to combine work and study more easily. In this context it should also be noted that far more young people are enrolling for degrees with the Open University (*Guardian* 2002).
7 The University of Texas runs a well-regarded mentoring system which is directed towards those with family incomes of less than $35,000 (Ehrenberg 2007).

Appendix: The West of Scotland study

1 Carstairs and Morris (1991) construct their scale using levels of male unemployment, overcrowding, low social class and car ownership to classify every postcode sector in Scotland on a scale from DEPCAT 1 (most affluent) to DEPCAT 7 (most deprived).

References

Acker, S. (1980) Women in higher education: what is the problem?, in S. Acker and P.D. Warren (eds) *Is Higher Education Fair to Women?* London: SHRE/ NFER-Nelson.

Adnett, N. and Slack, K. (2007) Are there economic incentives for non-traditional students to enter HE? The labour market as a barrier to widening participation, *Higher Education Quarterly*, 61(1): 23–36.

Allen, M. and Ainley, P. (2007) *Education Make You Fick, Innit? What's Gone Wrong in England's Schools, Colleges and Universities and How to Start Putting it Right.* London: Tufnell Press.

Archer, L. (2003) The 'value' of higher education, in L. Archer, M. Hutchings and A. Ross (eds) *Higher Education and Social Class: Issues of Exclusion and Inclusion.* London: RoutledgeFalmer.

Archer, L., Hutchings, M., Leathwood, C. and Ross, A. (2003) Widening participation in higher education: implications for policy and practice, in L. Archer, M. Hutchings and A. Ross (eds) *Higher Education and Social Class: Issues of Exclusion and Inclusion.* London: RoutledgeFalmer.

Ashton, D.N. and Field, D. (1976) *Young Workers.* London: Hutchinson.

Audas, R. and Dolton, P. (1999) Fleeing the nest, paper presented at the Royal Economics Society annual conference, Nottingham, 29 March to 1 April.

Baird, K. (2002) *An Inquiry into Withdrawal from College: A Study Conducted at Trinity College Dublin.* Dublin: Trinity College.

Baker, S. and Brown, B.J. (2007) *Rethinking Universities.* Bristol: Continuum.

Ball, S.J. (1981) *Beachside Comprehensive: A Case Study of Secondary Schooling.* Cambridge: Cambridge University Press.

Ball, S.J., Maguire, M. and Macrae, S. (2000) *Choice, Pathways and Transitions Post-16.* London: RoutledgeFalmer.

Ball, S.J., Reay, D. and David, M. (2002) 'Ethnic choosing': minority ethnic students, social class and higher education choice, *Race, Ethnicity and Education*, 5: 333–57.

Barke, M., Braidford, P., Houston, M., Hunt, A., Lincoln, I., Morphet, C., Stone, I. and Walker, A. (2000) *Students in the Labour Market: Nature, Extent and Implications of Term Time Employment among University of Northumbria Undergraduates.* Research Report no. 215. London: DfEE.

Barnett, R. (2003) *Beyond All Reason: Living with Ideology in the University.* Buckingham: Open University Press.

√ Barr, J. (2008) *The Stranger Within: On the Idea of an Educated Public*. Rotterdam: Sense Publishers.

Barr, N. (2001) *The Welfare State as Piggy Bank: Information, Risk, Uncertainty and the Role of the State*. Oxford: Oxford University Press.

Baty, P. (2006) Litigation fear lets cheats off hook, *Times Higher Education Supplement*, 13 October.

Baum, S. and Payea, K. (2004) *Education Pays*. New York: College Board Publications.

Beck, U. (1992) *Risk Society: Towards a New Modernity*. London: Sage.

Beck, U. (2000) *The Brave New World of Work*. Cambridge: Polity.

Bennett, R. and Ali-Choudhury, R. (forthcoming) *Prospective Students' Perceptions of University Brands: An Empirical Study*. London: Centre for Research in Marketing, London Metropolitan University.

Berggren, C. (2008) Horizontal and vertical differentiation within higher education: gender and class perspectives, *Higher Education Quarterly*, 62(1/2): 20–39.

Biggart, A., Dobbie, F., Furlong, A., Given, L. and Jones, L. (2005) *24 in 2004: Findings from the Scottish School Leavers Survey*, Edinburgh: Scottish Executive.

Biggart, A. and Furlong, A. (1996) Educating 'discouraged workers': cultural diversity in the upper secondary school, *British Journal of Sociology of Education*, 17(3): 253–66.

Blackmore, J. (1997) Disciplining feminism: a look at gender equality struggles in Australian higher education, in L.G. Roman and L. Eyre (eds) *Dangerous Territories: Struggles for Difference and Equality in Education*. New York: Routledge.

Blanden, J., Gregg, P. and Machin, S. (2005) *International Mobility in Europe and North America*. London: Centre for Economic Performance.

Blanden, J. and Machin, S. (2004) Educational inequality and the expansion of UK higher education, *Scottish Journal of Political Economy*, 51(2): 230–49.

Blondal, S., Field, S. and Girouard, N. (2002) *Investment in Human Capital through Post-Compulsory Education, Efficiency and Equity Aspects*. Paris: OECD.

Bonham, B.S. (2005) Educational mobility in the USA through the community college transfer function, in J. Gallacher and M. Osborne (eds) *A Contested Landscape: International Perspectives on Diversity in Mass Higher Education*. Leicester: NIACE.

Bourdieu, P. (1977) Cultural reproduction and social reproduction, in J. Karabel and A.H. Halsey (eds) *Power and Ideology in Education, Society and Culture*. London: Sage.

Bourdieu, P. (1996) *The State Nobility: Elite Schools in the Field of Power*. Cambridge: Polity Press.

Bourdieu, P. and Wacquant, L. (1992) *Invitation to Reflexive Sociology*. Chicago: University of Chicago Press.

Bourgeois, E., Duke, C., Guyot, J.L. and Merrill, B. (1999) *The Adult University*. Buckingham: Society for Research into Higher Education/Open University Press.

Bowl, M. (2003) *Non-Traditional Entrants to Higher Education: They Talk about People Like Me*. Stoke-on-Trent: Trentham Books.

Brennan, J. and Naidoo, R. (2007) Higher education and the achievement (or prevention) of equity and social justice, in European Science Foundation (ed.) *Higher Education: Looking Forward*. Strasbourg: European Science Foundation.

Brennan, J. and Osborne, M. (2008) Higher education's many diversities: of students, institutions and experiences and outcomes?, *Research Papers in Education*, 23(2): 179–90.

Brennan, J. and Shah, T. (2003) *Access to What? Converting Educational Opportunity into*

Employment Opportunity. London: Centre for Higher Education Research and Information.

Brooks, K. (2007) Talking through transition: students' talk and investments in campus culture, paper presented at University Life Uncovered conference, Manchester, 9 November.

Brown, P. (1995) Cultural capital and social exclusion: some observations on recent trends in education, employment and the labour market, *Work, Employment and Society*, 9(1): 29–51.

Brown, P., Hesketh, A. and Williams, S. (2003) Employability in a knowledge-driven economy, *Journal of Education and Work*, 16(2): 107–26.

Burnhill, P. (1984) The ragged edge of compulsory schooling, in D. Raffe (ed.) *Fourteen to Eighteen: The Changing Pattern of Schooling in Scotland.* Aberdeen: Aberdeen University Press.

Calhoun, C. (2006) The university and the public good, *Thesis Eleven*, 84(1): 7–43.

Callender, C. (2003) *Attitudes to Debt: School Leavers and Further Education Students' Attitudes to Debt and Their Impact on Participation in Higher Education.* London: Universities UK.

Callender, C. and Jackson, J. (2005) Does the fear of debt deter students from higher education?, *Journal of Social Policy*, 34(4): 509–40.

Callender, C. and Kemp, M. (2000) *Changing Student Finances: Income, Expenditure and Take up of Student Loans among Full- and Part-time Higher Education Students in 1998/ 9*, Research Report RR 213. London: Department of Education and Employment.

Callender, C. and Wilkinson, D. (2003) *2002/03 Student Income and Expenditure Survey: Students' Income, Expenditure and Debt in 2002/03 and Changes since 1998/99.* Sheffield: Department of Education and Skills.

Carstairs, V. and Morris, R. (1991) *Deprivation and Health in Scotland.* Aberdeen: Aberdeen University Press.

Cartmel, F. and Furlong, A. (2000) *Youth Unemployment in Rural Areas.* York: York Publishing.

Chapman, B. and Ryan, C. (2002) Income contingent financing of student higher education charges: assessing the Australian innovation, *Welsh Journal of Education*, 11(1): 64–81.

Chester, J. and Bekhradnia, B. (2008) *Financial Support in English Universities: The Case for a National Bursary System.* Oxford: Higher Education Policy Institute.

Christie, H. and Munro, M. (2003) The logic of loans, *British Journal of Sociology of Education*, 24(5): 621–36.

Christie, H., Munro, M. and Wager, F. (2005) 'Day Students' in higher education: widening access students and successful transitions to university, *International Studies in Sociology of Education*, 15(1): 3–29.

Committee on Higher Education (1963) *Higher Education: Report of the Committee Appointed by the Prime Minister under the Chairmanship of Lord Robbins, 1961–63*, Cm 2154. London: HMSO.

Conlon, G. and Chevalier, A. (2002) *Rates of Return to Education: A Summary of Recent Evidence.* London: Centre for the Economics of Education, London School of Economics.

Connor, H., Burton, R., Pearson, R., Pollard, E. and Reagan, J. (1999) *Making the Right Choice: How Students Choose Universities and Colleges.* London: Universities UK.

Connor, H., Dewson, S., Tyers, C., Eccles, J., Regan, J. and Aston, J. (2001) *Social Class and Higher Education: Issues Affecting Decisions on Participation by Lower Social Class Groups.* London: Department for Education and Skills.

Connor, H., Tyres, C., Modood, T. and Hillage, J. (2004) *Why the Difference? A Closer Look at Higher Education Minority Ethnic Students and Graduates.* DfES Research Report RR552, London: DfES.

Cooke, R., Barkham, M., Audin, K., Bradley, M. and Davy, J. (2004) How social class differences affect students' experience of university, *Journal of Further and Higher Education*, 28(4): 407–21.

Côté, J.E. and Allahar, A.L. (2007) *Ivory Tower Blues: A University System in Crisis.* Toronto: University of Toronto Press.

Crosland, S. (1982) *Tony Crosland.* London: Jonathan Cape.

Croxford, L., Howieson, C., Ianelli, C., Raffe, D. and Shapira, M. (2006) Trends in education and youth transitions across Britain 1984–2002, paper presented at the conference Education and Social Change in England, Wales and Scotland 1984–2002, University of Edinburgh, Edinburgh.

Croxford, L. and Raffe, D. (2005) Education markets and social class inequality: a comparison of trends in England, Scotland and Wales, Working Paper, University of Edinburgh, Centre for Educational Sociology.

Curtis, A. (2007) The importance of cultural and social capital for persistence and success in higher education, paper presented at University Life Uncovered conference, Manchester, 9 November.

Davies, P., Williams, J. and Webb, S. (1997) Access to higher education in the late twentieth century: policy, power and discourse, in J. Williams (ed.) *Negotiating Access to Higher Education: The Discourse of Selectivity and Equity.* Buckingham: Open University Press.

Davies, R. and Elias, P. (2003) *Dropping Out: A Study of Early Leavers from Higher Education*, Research Report RR386. London: Department for Education and Skills.

Dearden, L., McGranahan, L. and Sianesi, B. (2005) *Returns to Education for the Marginal Learners: Evidence from the BCS70.* London: Centre for the Economics of Education.

Dearing, R. (1997) *Higher Education in the Learning Society: Report of the National Committee of Inquiry into HE.* London: The Stationery Office.

Department for Education and Employment (1997) *Higher Education in the 21st Century.* London: DfEE.

Devine, F. (2004) *Class Practices: How Parents Help Their Children Get Good Jobs.* Cambridge: Cambridge University Press.

Education in the USA (2007) www.infozee.com/usa/expenses.htm (accessed 10 July 2007).

Education Research Services (2007) Education Research Services Bulletin, Winter http://e-r-s.org.uk/ers_newsletter_01.html.

Edwards, R. (1993) *Mature Women Students: Separating or Connecting Family and Education.* London: Taylor and Francis.

Ehrenberg, R. (2007) Reducing inequality in higher education, in S. Dickert-Conlin and R. Rubenstein (eds) *Economic Inequality and Higher Education.* New York: Russell Sage Foundation.

Elias, P. and Purcell, K. (2004) *The Earnings of Graduates in their Early Careers*, Research Paper No. 5. Warwick: Institute of Employment.

Elliott, L. and Atkinson, D. (1998) *The Age of Insecurity.* London: Verso.

Evans, K. (2002) Challenging inequality, choosing inclusion: higher education in changing social landscapes, in A. Hayton and A. Paczuska (eds) *Access, Participation and Higher Education: Policy and Practice.* London: Kogan Page.

Fearn, H. (2008) Makeover mania, *Times Higher Education*, 6 March.

Field, J. (2004) Articulation and credit transfer in Scotland: taking the academic high road or a sidestep in a ghetto, *Journal of Access Policy and Practice*, 1(2): 85–99.

Finch, J. (1984) *Education as Social Policy*. London: Longman.

Ford, J. (1969) *Social Class and the Comprehensive School*. London: Routledge and Kegan Paul.

Forsyth, A. and Furlong, A. (2000) *Socioeconomic Disadvantage and Access to Higher Education*. Bristol: Policy Press.

Forsyth, A. and Furlong, A. (2003) *Losing Out? Socioeconomic Disadvantage and Experience in Further and Higher Education*. Bristol: Policy Press.

Furlong, A. and Cartmel, F. (1997) *Young People and Social Change: Individualization and Risk in Late Modernity*. Buckingham: Open University Press.

Furlong, A. and Cartmel, F. (2005) *Graduates from Disadvantaged Families: Early Labour Market Experiences*. Bristol: Policy Press.

Furlong, A. and Cartmel, F. (2007) *Young People and Social Change: New Perspectives*. Maidenhead: Open University Press.

Furlong, A., Cartmel, F., Biggart, A., Sweeting, H. and West, P. (2003) *Reconceptualising Youth Transitions: Patterns of Vulnerability and Processes of Social Exclusion*. Edinburgh: Scottish Executive.

Furlong, A. and Kelly, P. (2005) The Brazilianization of youth transitions in Australia and the UK?, *Australian Journal of Social Issues*, 40(2): 207–25.

Gallacher, J. and Osborne, M. (2005a) *Diversity or Division? International Perspectives on the Contested Landscape of Mass Higher Education*. Leicester: National Institute for Adult and Continuing Education.

Gallacher, J. and Osborne, M. (2005b) The role of short-cycle higher education on the changing landscape of mass higher education: issues for consideration, in J. Gallacher and M. Osborne (eds) *A Contested Landscape: International Perspectives on Diversity in Mass Higher Education*. Leicester: NIACE.

Gallacher, J., Osborne, M. and Postle, G. (1996) Increasing and widening access to higher education: a comparative study of policy and provision in Scotland and Australia, *International Journal of Lifelong Education*, 15(6): 418–37.

Gilchrist, R., Phillips, D. and Ross, A. (2003) Participation and potential participation in UK higher education, in L. Archer, M. Hutchings and A. Ross (eds) *Higher Education and Social Class: Issues of Exclusion and Inclusion*. London: RoutledgeFalmer.

Goldhaber, D. and Peri, G.K. (2007) Community colleges, in S. Dickert-Conlin and R. Rubenstein (eds) *Economic Inequality and Higher Education*. New York: Russell Sage Foundation.

Goldrick-Rab, S. (2006) Following their every move: an investigation of social class differences in college pathways, *Sociology of Education*, 79(1): 61–79.

Goldthorpe, J.H., Lockwood, D., Bechhofer, F. and Platt, J. (1969) *The Affluent Worker in the Class Structure*. Cambridge: Cambridge University Press.

Goldthorpe, J.H. (in collaboration with Llewellyn, C. and Payne, C.) (1980) *Social Mobility and the Class Structure in Modern Britain*. Oxford: Clarendon Press.

Goldthorpe, J.H. and Mills, C. (2000) Trends in intergenerational class mobility in Britain in the late twentieth century, working paper, quoted in S. Aldridge (ed.) *Social Mobility: A Discussion Paper*. London: Performance and Innovation Unit.

Gordon, P., Aldrich, R. and Dean, D. (1991) *Education and Policy in England in the Twentieth Century*. London: Woburn Press.

Green, A., Wolf, A. and Leney, T. (1999) *Convergence and Divergence in European Education and Training Systems*, Bedford Way Papers, No. 7, London: Institute of Education.

Greenwood, D.J. (2007) Who are the real problem owners? in A. Harding, A. Scott, S. Laske and C. Burtscher (eds) *Bright Satanic Mills*. Aldershot: Ashgate.

Guardian, The (2002) OU attracting more young people, 27 December.

Guardian, The (2004a) Black mark, 7 January.

Guardian, The (2004b) Oxford attack on admission reforms, 13 May.

Guardian, The (2005) Graduates turn back on buoyant job market, 10 February.

Guardian, The (2007) A foot in the door, 6 November.

Guardian, The (2008a) Where your money goes: the definitive atlas of UK government spending, 13 September.

Guardian, The (2008b) Universities urged to back more academies to reduce class bias, 11 February.

Halsey, A.H., Heath, A. and Ridge, J. (1980) *Origins and Destinations: Family, Class and Education in Modern Britain*. Oxford: Clarendon.

Harvey, L. and Drew, S. (with Smith, M.) (2006) *The First Year Experience: A Review of Literature for the Higher Education Academy*. York: Higher Education Academy.

Haveman, R. and Wilson, K. (2007) Access, matriculation and graduation, in S. Dickert-Conlin and R. Rubenstein (eds) *Economic Inequality and Higher Education*. New York: Russell Sage Foundation.

Heath, A. (1987) Class in the classroom, *New Society*, 17 July, pp. 13–15.

Heath, A. and Payne, C. (2000) Social mobility, in A.H. Halsey and J. Webb (eds) *Twentieth Century British Social Trends*. Basingstoke: Macmillan.

Heckman, J.J. and LaFontaine, P.A. (2007) *The American High School Graduation Rate: Trends and Levels*. Discussion Paper No. 3216. Bonn: Forschungsinstitut zur Zukunft der Arbeit (Institute for the Study of Labour).

HEFCE (Higher Education Funding Council for England) (2007) National Student Survey http://www.hefce.ac.uk/news/hefce/2007/nss.htm.

Heller, D. (2004) Pell Grant recipients in selected colleges and universities, in R. Kahlenberg (ed.) *America's Untapped Resource: Low Income Students in Higher Education*. New York: Century Foundation Press.

HESA (Higher Education Statistics Agency) (2007a) Participation of under-represented groups in first degree courses from low participation neighbourhoods by subject and entry qualification 2005/06. Available at: www.hesa.ac.uk/pi/0405/t1b_0405.xls (accessed 4 May 2007).

HESA (Higher Education Statistics Agency) (2007b) Career progression of graduates, Key findings, Press release 116, November. Available at: http://www.hesa.ac.uk/index.php/content/view/888/161/

HESA (Higher Education Statistics Agency) (2007c) Graduate unemployment under 6% for those with best degrees, Press release 114, August. Available at: http://www.hesa.ac.uk/index.php/content/view/778/161/

HESA (Higher Education Statistics Agency) (2008) Students in higher education institutions, 1994–2006. Available at: http://www.hesa.ac.uk/index.php/component/option,com_pubs/Itemid,122/#item1709 (accessed 15 October 2008).

Hill, D. (2003) Global neo-liberalism, the deformation of education and resistance, *Journal of Critical Education Policy Studies*, 1(1). Available at: http://www.jceps.com/index.php?pageID=article&articleID=7 (accessed 15 July 2008).

Hillage, J. and Pollard, E. (1998) *Employability: Developing a Framework for Policy*

Analysis, DfEE Research Briefing No. 85. London: Department for Education and Employment.

Hinton-Smith, T. (2006) Lone parents as HE students, paper presented at European Society for Research on the Education of Adults (ESREA) conference, University of Warwick, 7–8 December.

Hinton-Smith, T. (2007) Lone parents as higher education students, paper presented at University Life Uncovered conference, Manchester, 9 November.

Hobhouse, L.T. (1964) *Liberalism*. New York: Oxford University Press.

Hutchings, M. (2003) Information, advice and cultural discourses of higher education, in L. Archer, M. Hutchings and A. Ross (eds) *Higher Education and Social Class: Issues of Exclusion and Inclusion*. London: RoutledgeFalmer.

Hutton, W. (2006) The British middle class is operating a closed shop, *The Observer*, 18 June.

Iannelli, C. (2007) Inequalities in entry to higher education: a comparison over time between Scotland and England and Wales, *Higher Education Quarterly*, 61(3): 306–33.

Independent Committee of Inquiry into Student Finance (1999) *Student Finance: Fairness for the Future, Research Report:* Volume I, *Annexes J–M*. Edinburgh: Scottish Executive.

Jackson, B. and Marsden, D. (1966) *Education and the Working Class*. London: Routledge.

Journal of Blacks in Higher Education (2008) Despite surging endowments, high-ranking universities and universities show disappointing results in enrolling low-income students, September. Available at: www.jbhe.com/features/57_pellgrants.html (accessed 15 September 2008).

Karabel, J. (2005) *The Chosen: The Hidden History of Admission and Exclusion at Harvard, Yale and Princeton*. New York: Houghton Mifflin.

Keep, E. (2004) After access: researching labour market issues, in M. Osborne, J. Gallacher and B. Crossan (eds) *Researching Widening Access to Lifelong Learning*. London: RoutledgeFalmer.

Kirkup, G. (1996) The importance of gender, in R. Mills and A. Tait (eds) *Supporting the Learner in Open and Distance Learning*. London: Pitman.

Lampl, P. (2007) You say dropouts, but I say lifelong learners, *The Times Higher*, 26 October.

Lea, S.E., Webley, P. and Bellamy, G. (2001) Student debt: expecting it, spending it and regretting it, in A.J. Scott, A. Lewis and S. Lea (eds) *Student Debt: The Causes and Consequences of Undergraduate Borrowing in the UK*. London: Polity Press.

Leadiwood, C. and O'Connell, P. (2003) It's a struggle: the construction of the 'new student' in higher education, *Journal of Education Policy*, 18(6): 597–615.

Leathwood, C. (2006) Accessing higher education: policy, practice and equity in widening participation in England, in I. McNay (ed.) *Beyond Higher Education: Building on Experience*. Maidenhead: The Society for Research into Higher Education and Open University Press.

Leitch Report (2006) *Prosperity for All in the Global Economy: World Class Skills*. London: HMSO.

Little, B. (2006) The student experience and the impact of social capital, in I. McNay (ed.) *Beyond Mass Higher Education: Building on Experience*. Maidenhead: The Society for Research into Higher Education and Open University Press.

Maassen, P. and Cloete, N. (2006) Global reform trends in higher education, in N. Cloete, P. Maassen, R. Fehnel, T. Moja, T. Gibbon and H. Perold (eds) *Transformation in Higher Education*. Amsterdam: Springer.

Macrae, S. and Maguire, M. (2002) 'Getting in, getting on: choosing the best', in A. Hayton and A. Paczuska (eds) *Access, Participation and Higher Education*. London: Kogan Page.

Marks, A., Turner, E. and Osborne, M. (2003) 'Not for the likes of me': the overlapping effect of social class and gender factors in the decisions made by adults not to participate in higher education, *Journal of Further and Higher Education*, 27(4): 347–64.

Markus, H. and Nurius, P. (1986) Possible selves, *American Psychologist*, 41(9): 954–69.

McInnis, C., James, R. and Hartley, R. (2000) *Trends in First Year Experience of Australian Undergraduates*. Canberra: Australian Government Printing Service.

McIntosh, S. (2004) *Further Analysis of the Returns to Academic and Vocational Qualifications*. Research Report RR370. London: Department of Education and Skills.

MacLennan, A., Musselbrook, K. and Dundas, M. (2000) *Credit Transfer at the FE/HE Interface*. Edinburgh: Scottish Higher Education Funding Council/Scottish Further Education Funding Council.

McNay, I. (2006) The agenda ahead: building on experience, in I. McNay (ed.) *Beyond Mass Higher Education: Building on Experience*. Maidenhead: The Society for Research into Higher Education and Open University Press.

McPherson, M. and Schapiro, M. (1999) *Reinforcing Stratification in American Higher Education: Some Disturbing Trends*. Stanford, CA: National Center for Postsecondary Improvement, Stanford University.

Ministry of Education (1946) *Scientific Manpower*, The Barlow Report, Cm 6824. London: HMSO.

Ministry of Education (1960) *Grants to Students*, The Anderson Report, Cm 1051. London: HMSO.

Ministry of Education (1962) *Statistics of Education*. London: HMSO.

Minogue, K.R. (1973) *The Concept of University*. London: Weidenfeld and Nicholson.

Mitton, L. (2007) Means-tested higher education? The English university bursary mess, *Journal of Further and Higher Education*, 31(4): 373–83.

Modood, T. (2006) Ethnicity, Muslims and higher education entry in Britain, *Teaching in Higher Education*, 11(2): 247–50.

Moreau, M-P. and Leathwood, C. (2006) Graduates employment and the discourse of employability: a critical analysis, *Journal of Education and Work*, 19(4): 305–24.

MORI (2005) *The Student Experience Report 2005*. London: Higher Education Policy Unit.

National Audit Office (2002) *Widening Participation in Higher Education in England*. London: The Stationery Office.

National Audit Office (2007) *Staying the Course: The Retention of Students in Higher Education*. London: The Stationery Office.

NatWest Bank (2006) www.natwest.com/global-options.asp?id=global/media/131 (accessed 11 July 2007).

NatWest (2007) Student Money Matters. Available at: http://www.natwest.com/global_options.asp?id=GLOBAL/MEDIA/151 (accessed 04 November 2007).

National Statistics (2008) National Statistics Online. Available at: www.statistics.gov.uk/cci/nugget.asp?id=268 (accessed 26 February 2008).

Naylor, R., Smith, J. and McKnight, A. (2002) Sheer class? The extent and sources of variation in the UK graduate earning premium, CASE paper No. 54. London: Centre for Analysis of Social Exclusion, London School of Economics.

Newman, J.H. (1907) *The Idea of a University*. London: Longmans Green and Co.

Nurmi, J-E., Aunola, K., Salmela-Aro, K. and Lindroos, M. (2003) The role of success expectation and task avoidance in academic performance and satisfaction: three studies on antecedents, consequences and correlates, *Contemporary Educational Psychology*, 28(1): 59–90.

Nurmi, J-E., Salmela-Aro, K. and Koivisto, P. (2002) Goal importance and related achievement beliefs and emotions during the transition from vocational school to work: antecedents and consequences, *Journal of Vocational Behavior*, 60(2): 241–61.

Organisation for Economic Co-operation and Development (OECD) (2004) *Education at a Glance*. Paris: OECD.

Organisation for Economic Co-operation and Development (OECD) (2006) *Education at a Glance*. Paris: OECD.

Organisation for Economic Co-operation and Development (OECD) (2007) *Education at a Glance*. Paris: OECD.

Osborne, M. (2003) Increasing or widening participation in higher education?: A European overview, *European Journal of Education*, 38(1): 5–24.

Osborne, M., Marks, A. and Turner, E. (2004) Becoming a mature student: how adult applicants weigh the advantages and disadvantages of higher education, *Higher Education*, 48(3): 291–315.

Osborne, M. and McLaurin, I. (2006) A probability matching approach to Further Education/Higher Education transition in Scotland, *Higher Education*, 52(1): 149–83.

Osborne, M. and Young, D. (2006) *Flexibility and Widening Participation*. London: Higher Education Academy, Education Subject Centre. Available at: http://escalate.ac.uk/2499 (accessed 21 October 2008).

Ostrove, J.M. (2003) Belonging and wanting: meanings of social class background for women's constructions of their college experiences, *Journal of Social Issues*, 59(4): 771–84.

Ozga, J. and Sukhnanadan, L. (1998) Undergraduate non-completion: developing and explanatory model, *Higher Education Quarterly*, 52(3): 316–33.

Parjanen, M. and Tuomi, O. (2003) Access to higher education – persistent or changing inequality?: A case study from Finland, *European Journal of Education*, 38(1): 55–70.

Parkin, F. (1972) *Class Inequality and the Political Order: Social Stratification in Capitalist and Communist Societies*. London: Paladin.

Pearson, R., Aston, J., Bates, P. and Jagger, N. (2000) *The IES Annual Graduate Review 2000: A Diverse and Fragmented Market*. Report 367. Brighton: Institute of Employment Studies.

Perry, C. and Allard, A. (2003) Making the connections: transitional experiences for first year education students, *Journal of Educational Enquiry*, 4(2): 74–89.

PricewaterhouseCoopers (2007) *The Economic Benefits of a Degree*. London: Universities UK.

Purcell, K., Elias, P., Davies, R. and Wilton, N. (2005) *The Class of '99: A Study of the Early Labour Market Experiences of Recent Graduates*. London: Department for Education and Skills.

Purcell, K., Elias, P. and Wilton, N. (2004) Higher education, skills and employment: careers and jobs in the graduate labour market, researching graduate careers seven years on project. Research Paper No. 3. Warwick: Institute of Employment.

Quinn, J., Thomas, L., Slack, K., Casey, L., Thexton, W. and Noble, J. (2005) *From Life*

Crisis to Lifelong Learning: Rethinking Working-class 'Drop out' from Higher Education. York: Joseph Rowntree Foundation.

Raffe, D. and Willms, J.D. (1989) Schooling the discouraged worker: labour market effects on educational participation, *Sociology*, 23(4): 559–81.

Raftery, A.E. and Hout, M. (1993) Maximally maintained inequality: expansion, reform and opportunity in Irish education 1921–1975, *Sociology of Education*, 66(1): 41–62.

Rawls, J. (1971) *A Theory of Social Justice.* Oxford: Oxford University Press.

Reay, D. (2005) Who goes where in higher education: an issue of class, ethnicity and increasing concern. London: Institute for Policy Studies in Education, London Metropolitan University. Seminar paper presented at University of Birmingham, February 2005. Available at: http://asp.wlv.ac.uk/Level3.asp?UserType=11&Level3=1659.

Reay, D. (2007) An insoluble problem? Social class and English higher education, in R. Teese, S. Lamb and M. Duru-Dellat (eds) *International Studies in Educational Inequality, Theory and Practice.* Amsterdam: Springer.

Reay, D., David, M.E. and Ball, S. (2005) *Degrees of Choice: Class, Race, Gender and Higher Education.* Stoke on Trent: Trentham Books.

Rickinson, B. and Rutherford, D. (1995) Increasing undergraduate student retention rates, *British Journal of Guidance and Counselling*, 23(2): 161–72.

Rikowski, G. (2000) Education and social justice within the social universe of capital, paper presented at the British Educational Research Association seminar on Approaching Social Justice: Theoretical Frameworks and Practical Purpose. Available at: www.leeds.ac.uk/educol/documents/00001618.htm (accessed 15 July 2008).

Rosenbaum, J.E. (2002) *Beyond Empty Promises: Policies to Improve Transitions into College and Jobs* (ED-99-CO-0160). Washington, DC: U.S. Department of Education, Office of Vocational and Adult Education.

Ross, A. (2003a) Higher education and social access: to the Robbins report, in L. Archer, M. Hutchings and A. Ross (eds) *Higher Education and Social Class: Issues of Exclusion and Inclusion.* London: RoutledgeFalmer.

Ross, A. (2003b) Access to higher education: inclusion for the masses?, in L. Archer, M. Hutchings and A. Ross (eds) *Higher Education and Social Class: Issues of Exclusion and Inclusion.* London: RoutledgeFalmer.

Royal Bank of Scotland (2007) *Student Living Index: 2007.* Edinburgh: Royal Bank of Scotland. Available at: http://www.rbs.co.uk/content/personal/current_accounts/student/downloads/RBS_Student_Living_Index.pdf (accessed 12 August 2008).

Sastry, T. and Bekhradnia, B. (2007) *The Academic Experience of Students in English Universities.* London: Higher Education Policy Institute.

Saunders, P. (1996) *Unequal but Fair: A Study of Class Barriers in Britain.* London: Institute for Economic Affairs.

Scanlon, L., Rowling, L. and Weber, Z. (2007) You don't have like and identity . . . you are just lost in a crowd: forming a student identity in the first year transition to university, *Journal of Youth Studies*, 10(2): 223–41.

Scotland on Sunday (2005) Glasgow's schools fail in postcode lottery, 6 February.

Scottish Funding Council (2007) *Articulation for All?* Edinburgh: Scottish Funding Council.

Self, A. and Zealey, L. (eds) (2007) *Social Trends No. 37.* London: Office for National Statistics.

Sen, A. (1992) *Inequality Re-examined*. Oxford: Oxford University Press.

Shah, T. (2006) Affordability and accessibility, *International Higher Education*, 43, Spring. Available at: www.bc.edu/bc_org/avp/soe/cihe/newsletter/number43/p5_shah.htm (accessed 15 September 2008).

Shattock, M. (2006) United Kingdom, in J.F. Forest and P.G. Altbach (eds) *International Handbook of Higher Education:* Part Two, *Regions and Countries*. Amsterdam: Springer.

Shiner, M. and Modood, T. (2002) Help or hindrance? Higher education and the route to ethnic quality, *British Journal of Sociology of Education*, 23(2): 209–32.

Silver, H. (2007) *Tradition and Higher Education*. Winchester: Winchester University Press.

Skeggs, B. (1997) *Formations of Class and Gender: Becoming Respectable*. London: Sage.

Skilbeck, M. (2000) *Access and Equity in Higher Education*. Dublin: Higher Education Authority.

Smetherham, C. (2006) First among equals? Evidence on the contemporary relationships between educational credentials and the occupational structure, *Journal of Education and Work*, 19(1): 29–45.

Smith, A. and Webster, F. (1997) Changing ideas of the university, in A. Smith and F. Webster (eds) *The Postmodern University? Contested Visions of Higher Education in Society*. Buckingham: Open University Press.

Smith, J., McKnight, A. and Naylor, R. (2000) Graduate employability: policy and performance in higher education in the UK, *Economic Journal*, 110 (June): F382–F411.

Smith, J.P. and Naylor, R.A. (2001) Dropping out of university: a statistical analysis of the probability of withdrawal for UK university students, *Journal of the Royal Statistical Society, Series A*, 164(2): 389–405.

Sparrow, P.R. and Cooper, C.L. (2003) *The Employment Relationship: Key Challenges for HR*. Oxford: Butterworth-Heinemann.

Stone, J. III (2009) Keeping kids on track to a successful adulthood: the role of VET in improving high school outcomes, in A. Furlong (ed.) *Handbook of Youth and Young Adulthood*. London: Routledge.

Summerfield, C. and Gill, B. (eds) (2005) *Social Trends, No. 35*. London: Office for National Statistics.

Sunday Times (2008) The Sunday Times University Guide (supplement), 21 September.

Sutton Trust (2000) *Entry to Leading Universities*. London: The Sutton Trust.

Sutton Trust (2005a) *The Educational Backgrounds of Members of the House of Commons and House of Lords*. London: Sutton Trust.

Sutton Trust (2005b) *State School Admissions to Our Leading Universities*. London: The Sutton Trust.

Swartz, T.T and O'Brien, K.B. (2009) Intergenerational support during the transition to adulthood, in A. Furlong (ed.) *Handbook of Youth and Young Adulthood: New Perspectives and Agendas*. London: Routledge.

Teichler, U. (2004) Changing views in Europe about diversification in higher education, in S. Neaman Institute (ed.) *Transition to Mass Higher Education Systems: International Comparisons and Perspectives*. Haifa: S. Neaman Press.

Teichler, U. (2007) Does higher education matter? Lessons from a comparative graduate survey, *European Journal of Education*, 42(1): 10–34.

Telegraph, The (2001) Oxbridge interviews rude and aggressive, 2 December. Available at: http://www.telegraph.co.uk/education/main.jhtml?xml=/education/2001/12/08/tepoxb08.xml (accessed 22 October 2008).

Thomas, E. (2001) *Widening Participation in Post-Compulsory Education*. London: Continuum.

Thomas, L., May, H., Harrop, H., Houston, M., Knox, H., Lee, M.F., Osborne, M., Pudner, H. and Trotman, C. (2005) *From the Margins to the Mainstream*. London: UUK/SCOP.

Thomas, L., Quinn, J., Slack, K. and Casey, L. (2002) *Student Services: Effective Approaches to Retaining Students in Higher Education*. Staffordshire University: Institute for Access Studies.

Times, The (2008) Cambridge University's Alison Richard condemns push for state pupils, 10 September. Available at: www.timesonline.co.uk/tol/life_and_style/education/article4720330.ece?print=y (accessed 16 September 2008).

Times Higher, The (2008a) The week in higher education, 9 October.

Times Higher, The (2008b) Reform unfair aid system, says HEPI, 18 September.

Times Higher, The (2008c) Bigger than the Beatles, 7 February.

Times Higher, The (2008d) Undergraduate courses get chop, 2 October.

Times Higher Education Supplement, The (2007a) Diversity and challenge, 17 January.

Times Higher Education Supplement, The (2007b) Social life high on wish list, 7 December.

Times Higher Education Supplement, The (2007c) Class sizes spark fears over quality, 4 May.

Tinto, V. (1975) Dropout from higher education: a theoretical synthesis of recent research, *Review of Educational Research*, 45(1): 89–125.

Tinto, V. (1987) *Leaving College: Rethinking the Causes and Cures of Student Attrition*. Chicago: University of Chicago Press.

Tinto, V. (1993) *Leaving College: Rethinking the Causes and Cures of Student Attrition*, 2nd edn. Chicago: University of Chicago Press.

Trow, M. (2006) Reflection on the transition from elite to mass to universal education access: forms and phases of higher education in modern societies since WWII, in J. James, F. Forest, G. Phillip and P. Altbach (eds) *International Handbook of Higher Education*. Amsterdam: Springer.

Tysome, T. (2002) 'Unwashed' must brush up on their social skills, *Times Higher Educational Supplement*, 17 May.

UCAS (2007) www.ucas.ac.uk/figures/ucasdata/ethnicity/index.html (accessed 4 May 2007).

Universities UK (2007) *Research Report: The Economic Benefits of a Degree*. London: Universities UK.

Usher, A. (2005) *Global Debt Patterns: An International Comparison of Student Loan Burdens and Repayment Conditions*. Toronto: Education Policy Institute.

Välimaa, J. and Hoffman, D. (2007) Higher education and knowledge society discourse, in European Science Foundation (ed.) *Higher Education: Looking Forward*. Strasbourg: European Science Foundation.

Wakeling, P. (2005) La noblesse d'état anglaise? Social class and progress to postgraduate study, *British Journal of Sociology of Education*, 26(4): 505–22.

Washington Post (2007) Bush's 2008 budget calls for boost to Pell Grant, 2 February.

Watson, D. (2006) How to think about widening participation in UK higher education. Discussion paper prepared for HEFCE. Available at: www.hefce.ac.uk/pubs/rdreports/2006/rd13-06/think.doc (accessed 24 November 2006).

Wisker, G. (1996) *Empowering Women in Higher Education*. London: Kogan Page.

Wooden, M. and Warren, D. (2003) *The Characteristics of Casual and Fixed-term Employ-*

ment: Evidence from the HILDA Survey. Melbourne: Institute for Applied Economic and Social Research.

Wyn, J. (2009) Educating for late modernity, in A. Furlong (ed.) *Handbook of Youth and Young Adulthood: New Perspectives and Agendas.* London: Routledge.

Yale School of Forestry and Environmental Studies (1997) School website. Available at: http://environment.yale/edu/doc/1424/tuition_fees_and_other_expenses/ (accessed 10 July 2007).

Yorke, M. and Longden, B. (2008) *The First Year Experience of Higher Education in the UK.* London: The Higher Education Academy.

Young, M. (1958) *The Rise of the Meritocracy.* London: Thames and Hudson.

Young, M. (1961) *The Rise of the Meritocracy*, 2nd edn. Harmondsworth: Penguin.

Zaijda, J., Majhanovich, S. and Rust, V. (2006) Introduction: education and social justice, *International Review of Education*, 52(1): 9–22.

Index

The Society for Research into Higher Education

The Society for Research into Higher Education (SRHE), an international body, exists to stimulate and coordinate research into all aspects of higher education. It aims to improve the quality of higher education through the encouragement of debate and publication on issues of policy, on the organization and management of higher education institutions, and on the curriculum, teaching and learning methods.

The Society is entirely independent and receives no subsidies, although individual events often receive sponsorship from business or industry. The Society is financed through corporate and individual subscriptions and has members from many parts of the world. It is an NGO of UNESCO.

Under the imprint *SRHE & Open University Press*, the Society is a specialist publisher of research, having over 80 titles in print. In addition to *SRHE News*, the Society's newsletter, the Society publishes three journals: *Studies in Higher Education* (three issues a year), *Higher Education Quarterly* and *Research into Higher Education Abstracts* (three issues a year).

The Society runs frequent conferences, consultations, seminars and other events. The annual conference in December is organized at and with a higher education institution. There are a growing number of networks which focus on particular areas of interest, including:

Access	FE/HE
Assessment	Graduate Employment
Consultants	New Technology for Learning
Curriculum Development	Postgraduate Issues
Eastern European	Quantitative Studies
Educational Development Research	Student Development

Benefits to members

Individual

- The opportunity to participate in the Society's networks
- Reduced rates for the annual conferences
- Free copies of *Research into Higher Education Abstracts*
- Reduced rates for *Studies in Higher Education*

- Reduced rates for *Higher Education Quarterly*
- Free online access to *Register of Members' Research Interests* – includes valuable reference material on research being pursued by the Society's members
- Free copy of occasional in-house publications, e.g. *The Thirtieth Anniversary Seminars Presented by the Vice-Presidents*
- Free copies of *SRHE News* and *International News* which inform members of the Society's activities and provides a calendar of events, with additional material provided in regular mailings
- A 35 per cent discount on all SRHE/Open University Press books
- The opportunity for you to apply for the annual research grants
- Inclusion of your research in the *Register of Members' Research Interests*

Corporate

- Reduced rates for the annual conference
- The opportunity for members of the Institution to attend SRHE's network events at reduced rates
- Free copies of *Research into Higher Education Abstracts*
- Free copies of *Studies in Higher Education*
- Free online access to *Register of Members' Research Interests* – includes valuable reference material on research being pursued by the Society's members
- Free copy of occasional in-house publications
- Free copies of *SRHE News* and *International News*
- A 35 per cent discount on all SRHE/Open University Press books
- The opportunity for members of the Institution to submit applications for the Society's research grants
- The opportunity to work with the Society and co-host conferences
- The opportunity to include in the *Register of Members' Research Interests* your Institution's research into aspects of higher education

Membership details: SRHE, 76 Portland Place, London W1B 1NT, UK Tel: 020 7637 2766. Fax: 020 7637 2781. email: srheoffice@srhe.ac.uk world wide web: http://www.srhe.ac.uk./srhe/ *Catalogue*: SRHE & Open University Press, McGraw-Hill Education, McGraw-Hill House, Shoppenhangers Road, Maidenhead, Berkshire SL6 2QL. Tel: 01628 502500. Fax: 01628 770224. email: enquiries@openup.co.uk – web: www.openup.co.uk